MENNONITE
FAMILY
RECIPES

Hope Helmuth

MENNONITE FAMILY RECIPES

AUTHENTIC MEALS *for* YOUR TABLE

HERALD
PRESS

Harrisonburg, Virginia

Herald Press
PO Box 866, Harrisonburg, Virginia 22803
www.HeraldPress.com

Library of Congress Cataloging-in-Publication Data
Names: Helmuth, Hope, author.
Title: Mennonite family recipes : authentic meals for your table / Hope
  Helmuth.
Description: Harrisonburg, Virginia : Herald Press, [2021] | Includes
  index.
Identifiers: LCCN 2021016320 | ISBN 9781513809427 (paperback)
Subjects: LCSH: Mennonite cooking. | LCGFT: Cookbooks.
Classification: LCC TX721 .H472 2021 | DDC 641.5/66--dc23
LC record available at https://lccn.loc.gov/2021016320

MENNONITE FAMILY RECIPES
© 2021 by Herald Press, Harrisonburg, Virginia 22803. 800-245-7894.
    All rights reserved.
Library of Congress Control Number: 2021016320
International Standard Book Number: 978-1-5138-0942-7 (paperback)
Printed in United States of America

On the cover (top left, moving clockwise): Friday Night Pizza (p. 127),
Steak and Cheese Subs (p. 140), Chocolate Cake (p. 214), Stromboli (p. 124),
Citrus Shrimp Kabobs (p. 196), Chocolate Zucchini Bars (p. 241), Taco Corn
Soup (p. 48), Cinnamon Rolls (p. 16), Herb Roasted Chicken Thighs and
Potatoes (p. 188), Crunchy Broccoli Salad (p. 67), Slow-Baked Macaroni
(p. 100), Peanut Butter Bars (p. 242), Grilled Mushrooms (p. 105), Maple
Pecan Pie (p. 234)

Photography: Sera Petras (pp. 6, 8, 266, 272); Lana Whetzel (pp. 5); all other
photos by Hope Helmuth. Illustrations pp. 261–63 : Margarita Miller / iStock /
Getty Images Plus

25 24 23 22 21   10 9 8 7 6 5 4 3 2 1

For my girls:
may you find joy in everyday cooking

Contents

Introduction

Hello! I am so glad you opened this book. I'm a stay-at-home housewife and mom. I have a passion for cooking, creating recipes, and entertaining guests. Cooking is truly one of my love languages. I just love to cook for my family and anyone who enters our home.

My husband, Joshua, and I and our children live in Virginia's Shenandoah Valley, where we are surrounded by our families and community, which are rich in our Mennonite faith. We live in a Swiss chalet that Joshua's grandfather built, nestled among pine trees with a river running through the property.

I grew up on a farm, helping my mom and dad work in our garden. I think it's important for younger generations to learn where their food comes from and how to cook wholesome meals. To be a good cook, you don't have to have a spacious kitchen with the most expensive tools. You need basic ingredients, a fridge, a stove, an oven, and a willing mind to learn.

As my mom says, "Half the taste of food is the presentation." I believe God gave us colorful fruits and vegetables for us to enjoy and to create beautiful things with. My mom taught me to create meals with color and that a sprig of parsley as a garnish can brighten up anything.

These recipes are a combination of what I grew up eating and new recipes I have created.

They are from scratch and can be made mostly with what is in your pantry or refrigerator. I'm a last-minute, practical cook, but I also like things to taste and look good. I don't claim to be an expert at cooking, but I want to share the recipes that my family enjoys.

I have a passion for my Mennonite heritage and want to help preserve it. I do think that my heritage of cooking is slowly being lost. The busyness that this era brings makes it hard to keep some traditions—like eating meals together as a family—alive. I encourage you to gather your family and friends around your table. Community is so important for your family's health. This era brings so much pressure to be doing all the things everyone else is doing. But a community environment is more important than all the scheduled activities. We need to teach our children how to rest and enjoy the small but important things in life—like gathering around a table and sharing a home-cooked meal with family and friends.

Last but not least, I am a follower of Christ. Without Jesus, I am nothing. May all the glory be given to God. More than anything, I desire to do God's will while I am on this earth. "Thou art worthy, O Lord, to receive glory and honour and power: for thou hast created all things, and for thy pleasure they are and were created" (Revelation 4:11 KJV).

With love,

Hope

Breakfast

I'm not a morning person. That's hard to admit, but I've decided to embrace that fact. Still, I try to be disciplined and to be cheerful in the mornings. So you'll understand why I don't fix elaborate breakfasts. We usually have fried *pon haus* (a mixture of broth, meat, and cornmeal that is sliced and then fried) or sausage and eggs. Some weekends I mix up waffle batter and use that same batter the whole weekend. It keeps just fine in the refrigerator. On special weekends, I make sausage gravy and fried apples.

But the most important thing? That hot coffee mug I hug while making breakfast.

Simple Granola

SERVES 6

This granola is great with milk or in a parfait with yogurt and fresh fruit. We give this granola to our Airbnb guests. They love it, and some even eat the whole jarful before they leave. I choose not to add dried fruit to my granola because my jaws get tired from chewing it! But you could add some dried fruit after the granola is baked and cooled.

6 cups rolled oats

1 cup chopped pecans

1½ cup shredded coconut

¼ cup butter, melted

½ cup canola oil

½ cup maple syrup

½ packed cup brown sugar

1½ teaspoon salt

1 teaspoon ground cinnamon

½ teaspoon vanilla extract

In a large mixing bowl, combine rolled oats, pecans, and coconut. In a separate bowl, mix together remaining ingredients. Pour over rolled oat mixture and mix well.

Pour granola onto a baking sheet lined with parchment paper. Spread out evenly. Bake at 300°F for 45–60 minutes, or just until golden brown (baking times seem to vary by oven in this recipe). Do not stir. Remove from oven and let cool completely. You will need to break the granola into smaller clumps for storage. Place in an airtight container to keep fresh.

Waffles

SERVES 6

These waffles are quick and delicious. You can mix them up the night before and refrigerate the batter overnight. The batter also works great for pancakes. If making several waffles at a time, heat your oven to 200°F and place the waffles in a single layer on a baking sheet in the oven while baking the remaining waffles. This helps them stay warm and crisp.

1 cup unbleached white flour

1 cup white whole wheat flour

1 tablespoon sugar

1 tablespoon baking powder

1 teaspoon salt

1¾ cup milk

2 eggs, beaten

¼ cup sour cream

¼ cup butter, melted

In a medium bowl, mix together the white flour, whole wheat flour, sugar, baking powder, and salt. Make a well in the center of the flour mixture; set aside. In another bowl, beat together milk, eggs, and sour cream. Pour milk mixture into flour mixture and mix just until combined (it's okay if there are some clumps). Fold in melted butter. Bake in hot waffle iron for waffles or on a griddle for pancakes.

Sausage Gravy

SERVES 4

If you want your family to jump out of bed in the morning, make sausage gravy. I serve it over pancakes, waffles, or biscuits.

1 pound ground
  pork sausage

½ cup unbleached white flour

4 cups milk

salt and pepper

In a large skillet, brown sausage. Stir in flour and keep stirring until most of it is dissolved. Pour in milk while stirring constantly. Simmer on low heat until gravy is thickened. Season to taste with salt and pepper. If the gravy is too thick, add more milk.

Fried Apples

SERVES 4 – 6

These are a tasty side to a savory breakfast dish. They are also good on waffles with sausage gravy. I like to use Gala apples.

¼ cup butter

6 apples, sliced

2 teaspoons lemon juice

⅓ packed cup brown sugar

¼ teaspoon salt

1 teaspoon ground cinnamon

dash ground nutmeg

In a cast iron skillet, melt butter and then add apples. Sprinkle apples with lemon juice, brown sugar, and salt. Cover and cook on medium-low for 10 minutes, or until apples are just tender. Remove lid and sprinkle cinnamon and nutmeg over top. If a lot of liquid remains, turn heat to high and cook liquid down until it reduces.

Cinnamon Rolls

with Caramel Icing

MAKES 3–4 DOZEN ROLLS

Cinnamon rolls, smothered with caramel icing, are a favorite of mine. Freeze them the same day you bake them—even if you plan to serve them the next day—so they retain their freshness. A day-old cinnamon roll just isn't the same! Also, be sure not to overbake them.

Rolls

2 cups warm water

¼ cup active dry yeast

1 tablespoon granulated sugar

¾ cup butter, softened

1 cup granulated sugar

4 eggs

2 teaspoons vanilla extract

1 tablespoon salt

8½ cups unbleached white flour

In a medium bowl, mix together water, yeast, and 1 tablespoon granulated sugar. Set aside.

Using a stand mixer fitted with the wire whip, cream together butter and 1 cup additional granulated sugar until fluffy. Add eggs, one at a time, then add vanilla and salt. Add yeast mixture. Switch to the dough hook attachment on your mixer; add flour. Knead until smooth. The dough will be sticky. Place dough in a greased large bowl and cover. Let rise until doubled.

Filling

½ cup butter, melted

⅔ cup brown sugar

2 tablespoons ground cinnamon

Divide dough in half. On floured surface, roll one half into a 12 x 24-inch rectangle. Spread half the melted butter on the first rectangle and sprinkle with half the brown sugar and cinnamon. Roll up lengthwise and pinch seams well. With a string, cut into rounds about 1 inch thick. Place in a greased 9 x 13-inch baking dish (or baking pan) and cover with a light cloth. Repeat this step for the remaining dough. Let rise until doubled, about 40 minutes. Bake at 350°F for 15–20 minutes, or until internal temperature reaches 190°F. The baking time may differ with your choice of pan or the thickness of the rolls.

Caramel icing

¾ cup butter

1½ cup brown sugar

⅔ cup milk

2 cups powdered sugar

1 teaspoon vanilla extract

pinch salt

In a saucepan, melt butter. Stir in brown sugar, bring to a boil, and boil for 1 minute. Add milk and return to a boil. Remove from heat. Cool 5 minutes. Add powdered sugar, vanilla, and salt. Whisk until smooth. Spread on warm rolls.

Fiesta Lime Omelet

SERVES 2

A flavor-filled omelet that Joshua loves. The combination of sour cream and salsa on eggs is simply wonderful.

3 slices bacon

¼ onion, sliced

½ jalapeño pepper, sliced

5 eggs

2 tablespoons milk

salt and pepper

1 lime, halved

½ cup shredded cheddar cheese

¼ cup sour cream

¼ cup salsa

fresh parsley or cilantro, for garnish

Use kitchen scissors to snip bacon into small pieces and drop in a nonstick skillet. Fry bacon on medium heat until almost done. Add onion and jalapeño pepper. Sauté until tender.

In a small bowl, beat eggs and milk, and sprinkle in a dash salt and pepper. Add egg mixture to skillet. Cover and cook on low until omelet is set. Squeeze juice of half a lime onto omelet. Then cover half the omelet with cheese. Using a spatula, fold in half.

Slide omelet onto a serving plate. Add a dollop of sour cream and salsa. Garnish with fresh parsley or cilantro, slice the remaining lime half into wedges, and serve.

Soft Baked Eggs

SERVES 4–6

An easy way to fix a dozen eggs for breakfast. It's simple and delicious.

1 pound ground pork sausage

1 cup shredded Monterey
  Jack cheese

12 eggs

½ cup heavy cream

salt and pepper

fresh basil, chopped

In a skillet, brown sausage. Spread browned sausage on the bottom of a 9 x 13-inch baking dish. Sprinkle with cheese and crack eggs on top, side by side. Pour heavy cream evenly over the eggs and sprinkle with a dash salt and pepper. Bake at 350°F for 15–20 minutes. Remove from oven before the eggs are set, because they will continue to cook. Sprinkle basil on top before serving.

Basic Quiche

SERVES 4–6

Quiche is delicious served hot or cold. I like how versatile it is. You can use different meats, vegetables, and cheeses. Just be sure to cook raw vegetables before adding them to the pie shell so the juices release before baking. You don't want a soggy quiche!

½ onion, sliced

2 cups spinach

1 (9-inch) unbaked pie shell

8 slices bacon, fried and chopped, or 1 cup
  ground pork sausage, browned

1½ cup shredded cheddar or Gouda cheese

3 eggs

2 cups half-and-half

½ teaspoon salt

freshly ground pepper, as desired

In a skillet, heat a little oil and sauté onions until translucent. Add spinach. Stir until wilted, then drain.

In an unbaked pie shell, layer spinach, onions, meat of choice, and cheese. In a small bowl, beat together eggs, half-and-half, salt, and pepper. Pour over mixture in pie shell. Bake at 375°F for 30 minutes. Let stand 10 minutes before slicing.

Sausage Potato Quiche

SERVES 4 – 6

I grew up eating this quiche for supper, not only breakfast. It's hearty and delicious.

Crust

3 cups uncooked shredded potatoes

½ cup chopped onion

3 tablespoons oil

In a small bowl, mix together shredded potatoes, onions, and oil. Press into a 9-inch deep-dish pie pan. Bake at 400°F until browned (about 12 minutes).

Filling

2 eggs, beaten

1 cup milk or cream

½ teaspoon salt

½ teaspoon pepper

2 cups ground pork sausage, browned

1½ cup shredded cheddar cheese

1 fresh tomato, chopped

1 tablespoon chopped fresh parsley, or 1 teaspoon dried parsley flakes

In a small bowl, beat eggs, milk, salt, and pepper.

Remove potato crust from the oven and sprinkle with browned sausage, cheese, and tomato. Pour egg mixture over top and sprinkle with parsley. Bake at 350°F for 40 minutes; let rest 5 minutes before serving so the egg mixture can set.

Potato Nest Skillet

I love fried potatoes for breakfast. You can also use leftover baked or roasted potatoes or pre-shredded hash browns. Sauté onions, then add precooked potatoes. Season with salt and pepper and skip ahead to making nests for the eggs.

2 tablespoons oil

3 medium potatoes, cut into thin
  matchsticks

¼ cup chopped onions

salt and pepper

6 eggs

¼ cup half-and-half

½ cup shredded Monterey Jack
  cheese

In a skillet, heat oil over medium heat. Add potatoes and onions. Stir often to prevent potatoes from sticking (if needed, add a little water to loosen up the pan bottom).

Once the potatoes are tender, sprinkle with salt and pepper and stir well. Then make six "nests" for the eggs. Crack an egg into each nest and sprinkle each egg yolk with a little additional salt. Top with half-and-half. Reduce heat to low, cover, and cook until eggs are almost set. Top with cheese. Turn off heat and cover again until the cheese is melted.

Breads

There is nothing like walking into a kitchen filled with the smell of freshly baked bread. I didn't bake bread until I got married, but I have learned over the years, by trial and error. Now I can bake bread that looks nice enough to give away.

I used to struggle with shaping my bread loaves and finally learned to roll out the dough as wide as my bread pan, brush the top with water, and roll it up like a jelly roll. These steps help ensure a nice inside texture free from air pockets.

When I bake bread, it seems half a loaf is eaten before that fresh-baked bread smell has even left my kitchen. But then I remember that's why I baked it in the first place: to nourish the ones I love.

Blueberry and White Chocolate Scones

MAKES 8 SCONES

This recipe is from a good friend, Amy, who makes the best scones. You can use other kinds of frozen fruit. Great for an afternoon coffee break on a rainy day.

2 cups unbleached white flour

⅓ cup sugar, plus additional for sprinkling

1 tablespoon baking powder

½ teaspoon salt

6 tablespoons cold butter, grated

½ cup frozen blueberries

¼ cup white chocolate chips

½–¾ cup heavy cream

In a medium bowl, mix together flour, ⅓ cup sugar, baking powder, and salt. Cut in grated butter and mix until coarse. Add blueberries and white chocolate chips. Using your hands to mix, add cream ¼ cup at a time until mixture comes together and forms a ball. Form dough into a 7-inch circle and wrap in plastic wrap. Refrigerate until stiff. Cut into 8 wedges. Place scones on baking sheet lined with parchment paper. Brush tops with heavy cream and sprinkle with additional sugar. Bake at 400°F for 15–18 minutes, or until starting to brown.

Aunt Shirley's Corn Bread

SERVES 8

This recipe is from my aunt Shirley. All who try it fall in love with the taste and texture.

1 cup unbleached white flour

¾ cup cornmeal

3 tablespoons sugar

1 teaspoon baking soda

1 teaspoon baking powder

½ teaspoon salt

2 eggs

1 cup sour cream

¾ cup buttermilk

2 tablespoons butter, melted

In a medium-sized bowl, mix together ingredients in order listed. Pour into a greased 9-inch cast iron skillet, 9-inch baking dish, or muffin cups. Bake at 350°F for 20–25 minutes (until wooden pick inserted in the center comes out clean), or 14 minutes for muffin cups. Serve warm with additional butter and honey.

Belizean Fry Jacks

SERVES 6

During my teenage years, a student from Belize named Lynette lived with my family. Years later, we consider her part of our family and I call her my sister. Lynette makes the best fry jacks. This dough also makes wonderful tortillas.

2 cups unbleached white flour
1½ teaspoon baking powder
½ heaping teaspoon salt
1 tablespoon cold butter
½–¾ cup cold water
canola oil, for frying

In a small bowl, mix together flour, baking powder, and salt with your hands. Cut in butter until largest pieces are the size of a pea. Add ½ cup cold water and keep stirring with your hands, adding just enough additional water for the dough to come together. Knead until smooth. The dough should be soft and elastic but not sticky. Form into 8 balls. Place in a container and cover. Refrigerate for 10–15 minutes or overnight.

In a medium-sized saucepan, heat 2 inches canola oil.

Using minimal flour, roll each ball into a thin circle. Cut into thirds. To test if the oil is hot enough, drop one piece of fry jack in the saucepan; if the dough doesn't bubble up right away or starts to sink, the oil is not hot enough. Once the oil is sufficiently hot, fry pieces on both sides until golden brown. Place in a bowl lined with paper towels. Serve immediately. Fry jacks are good with rice and chicken, or you can eat them with jam.

For tortillas:
After kneading, form dough into 6 balls. Place in fridge for 10–15 minutes or overnight. Using minimal flour, roll each ball into a thin circle. In hot skillet with a bit of oil, fry on each side until tortilla starts to bubble and brown. Remove from heat and cover with a heavy cloth while you make the rest.

French Bread

This is the first bread I tried to make when I was a young cook, and it's still a favorite of mine to make. This French bread is soft and fluffy, and it's hard to stop eating it when it's fresh out of the oven. I use this same dough for rolls and sandwich bread. It makes about 27 (2-ounce) rolls or 2 nice loaves of sandwich bread.

2½ cups warm water

2 tablespoons active dry yeast

2 tablespoons sugar

3 tablespoons butter, melted

2 teaspoons salt

1 tablespoon sunflower lecithin*
  (optional)

6–7 cups unbleached white flour

1 egg, beaten

1 tablespoon water

Using a stand mixer fitted with a dough hook, mix together warm water, yeast, and sugar. Let rest until yeast foams. Mix in melted butter, salt, and sunflower lecithin, if desired. With mixer on low, start adding flour 2 cups at a time. Mix until the dough pulls away from the sides of the mixing bowl and is smooth, about 5 minutes. Place dough in a greased large bowl; cover tightly with plastic wrap. Let rise until doubled in size, punch down, and let rise again until doubled in size.

Divide dough in half. Roll each half into a 10 x 14-inch rectangle. Brush outside edges with water. Roll up, and pinch seam edges tight. Place loaves seam side down on a greased baking sheet. Cover with a light cloth. Let rise until doubled in size.

In a small bowl, beat egg and water and then brush over loaf tops. Using a sharp knife, make six ¼-inch-deep diagonal slashes across the top of each loaf. Bake at 350°F for 25 minutes, or until the centers register 195°F. Remove from oven and brush tops with additional butter. Cool on wire racks. Cut into thick slices and serve.

*Lecithin increases tenderness and improves the shelf life of breads.

Easy Sourdough Bread

MAKES 2 SANDWICH BREAD LOAVES

This bread is wonderful and easy to make. Sourdough bread has a delightful chewy texture and a lovely tang at the end. The dough can be used for many other things. This recipe is tweaked from Glenda Groff's cookbook Around the Family Table. *Sourdough starter can be purchased online— better yet, ask for a starter from a friend who bakes with sourdough.*

2 cups unfed sourdough starter

1 cup water

½ cup milk

2 tablespoons butter, melted

2 tablespoons honey

5–5½ cups unbleached white flour

1 tablespoon sunflower lecithin*
   (optional)

2½ teaspoons salt

Using a stand mixer fitted with the dough hook, mix together the sourdough starter, water, milk, melted butter, honey, flour, and sunflower lecithin, if desired. Mix for 3 minutes, or knead by hand on a floured surface for the same amount of time. Cover the mixing bowl with a cloth and let dough rest for 30 minutes.

Uncover, add salt, and knead for 5 minutes more. Place dough in a greased large bowl. Cover tightly with lid or plastic wrap and let rise 4 hours. Follow steps for one of the options below.

For bread:

Divide dough in half, roll out, and shape into 2 loaves. Place in two greased bread pans. Place each loaf in a large plastic bag, securing the ends. Let rise until bread has risen about 1½ inch above the pan rim.

Remove plastic bags. Score loaves and bake at 375°F for 25–30 minutes, or until the centers register 195°F. Cool on baking racks and freeze one loaf for later in the week.

For a chewier artisan bread texture:

Divide dough in half, roll out, and shape into 2 loaves. Place each loaf in a large plastic bag and secure the ends. Refrigerate for 12 hours. Remove from refrigerator and let rise until dough has risen about 1½ inch above the pan rim.

Remove plastic bags. Score loaves and bake at 375°F for 25–30 minutes, or until the centers register 195°F.

For pizza:

Either proceed to make crust as instructed below or, for a chewier texture, place dough in a bowl covered with a lid and ferment for several days in the refrigerator. After the desired rise time, line two baking sheets with parchment paper and drizzle with olive oil. Divide the dough in half and press halves onto baking sheets, up to 1–2 inches away from the sides of the sheets. Top with pizza sauce, shredded mozzarella cheese, and toppings. Bake at 475°F for 12–15 minutes.

*Lecithin increases tenderness and improves the shelf life of breads.

Mom's Rolls

MAKES ABOUT 3 DOZEN ROLLS

These rolls were present all throughout my childhood. When company came, we served them with butter and jam. When we had youth parties, the rolls would be filled with shaved ham and cheese.

4 cups unbleached white flour

2 cups whole wheat flour

¾ cup sugar

2 teaspoons salt

1 cup warm water

1 tablespoon active dry yeast

1 cup mashed potatoes

½ cup lard or butter

3 eggs, beaten

In a large mixing bowl, combine white flour, wheat flour, sugar, and salt. Form a well and add warm water and yeast. Let stand until yeast foams.

In another mixing bowl, combine mashed potatoes (leftovers or instant mashed potatoes, prepared according to package directions), lard, and beaten eggs. Mix well. Add potato mixture to yeast mixture in well and mix until smooth. With a large wooden spoon, work in the flour. Let rise until doubled in size.

Roll dough out to ½ inch thick. Cut with a biscuit cutter. Place on a greased baking sheet and let rise until doubled. Bake at 350°F for 12 minutes. Brush with butter and cover with wax paper to soften tops. Cover with a cloth until cool.

Pretzel Buns

MAKES 12 BUNS

These buns change the hamburger game. Once you've had them, you can't make grilled burgers without them. Time is one of the most important ingredients. Five minutes can make a big difference. These buns do not keep well, so be sure to eat them fresh! This recipe can be used to make soft pretzels.

1½ cup warm water

1 tablespoon active dry yeast

⅓ cup brown sugar

¼ teaspoon salt

4 cups unbleached white flour

2 cups hot water

2 tablespoons baking soda

pretzel salt, for sprinkling

melted butter, for brushing tops

Using a stand mixer fitted with the dough hook, mix together warm water and yeast. Add brown sugar, salt, and flour. Knead on medium speed until dough is smooth and pulls away from the sides of the bowl, about 4–5 minutes. Cover and let rise 10 minutes. Divide dough into 12 even pieces and form into flat 3½-inch round buns. Mix together hot water and baking soda. Dip entire roll into soda mixture. After dipping buns in mixture, slash tops ⅛ inch deep. Lay on a parchment-lined baking sheet. Sprinkle pretzel salt on top. Bake at 375°F for 12 minutes. Brush with melted butter and serve immediately.

For soft pretzels:

Use ½–¾ cup more flour. If the dough is too sticky, it will be difficult to roll. Divide dough into 12 even pieces and roll into strands. Form into pretzel shapes and prepare as directed for buns.

Cheesy Breadsticks

SERVES 4

I've made this recipe many times for a Sunday evening snack for company. No one will turn down cheesy breadsticks!

1 cup warm water

1 tablespoon active dry yeast

1 tablespoon olive oil

1 tablespoon honey

2½ cups unbleached white flour

1 teaspoon salt

¼ teaspoon garlic powder

¼ teaspoon dried basil

¼ teaspoon dried oregano

⅛ teaspoon salt

several dashes pepper

2 tablespoons butter, melted

½ cup shredded mozzarella cheese

¼ cup freshly grated Parmesan cheese

1 pint (2 cups) pizza sauce

In a 2-cup liquid measuring cup, whisk together warm water, yeast, oil, and honey. In a medium bowl, combine flour and 1 teaspoon salt. Make a well in the middle of the flour and pour in the yeast mixture. Mix together with fork until combined. Knead lightly with your hands and form into a smooth ball. Cover and let rise 20 minutes.

Grease a 13 x 18-inch baking sheet and spread dough to within 1–2 inches of the sides of the baking sheet. In a small bowl, mix together garlic powder, dried basil, dried oregano, ⅛ teaspoon additional salt, and pepper. Brush dough with melted butter and sprinkle with seasonings mixture. Top with cheeses.

Let rise 15 minutes. Bake at 400°F for 15 minutes. With a pizza cutter, cut into breadsticks and serve warm with pizza sauce.

Soups

There is something comforting about warm soup on a cold day. It warms you to your core. In fact, it's hard not to label every winter day a "soup day"!

Soups can be considered a cook's "easy way out," since making soup can mean dumping leftovers in a pot and adding broth or milk. Yet there actually can be lots of love put into a pot of hearty, steaming soup, even one made from leftovers. Quality ingredients and spices can make a pot of soup really sing; when it's paired with homemade bread, you'll hear a harmonious chorus.

My family and I like hearty soups with lots of meat and vegetables. If you find my soups too "hearty," just add more of the liquid the recipe calls for, and be sure to adjust the salt. From the vegetable beef soup made from slow-roasted beef to the chicken noodle soup crafted with chicken broth made by simmering chicken bones for hours, nourishment awaits!

Bacon Corn Chowder

SERVES 4

This is one of Joshua's favorite soups. There is something special about bacon with corn.

6 slices bacon, chopped

1 large potato, diced (about 2 cups)

½ onion, diced

¼ cup white cooking wine

1 pint (2 cups) frozen corn, thawed

2 tablespoons butter

4 cups milk

2 tablespoons unbleached white
   flour

½ teaspoon salt

½ teaspoon pepper

½ teaspoon dried parsley flakes

In a soup pot, fry bacon until almost done. Drain off excess bacon drippings. Add diced potatoes and onions and fry until bacon is done and onions are translucent.

Add wine to deglaze pot. Stir until nothing is sticking to the bottom of the pot. Add corn and butter, cooking until butter is melted.

In a 4-cup liquid measuring cup, whisk together milk and flour until smooth and pour into pot. Add salt, pepper, and parsley flakes. Simmer on low heat for 10–15 minutes.

Zuppa Toscana

SERVES 4

This is a classic Italian soup. It's a good way to introduce your family to kale. They'll love it.

1 pound ground pork sausage

¼ teaspoon red pepper flakes

4 slices bacon, chopped

1 large onion, diced

4 garlic cloves, crushed

4 cups chicken stock

6 small red potatoes, cut into half-moon slices

salt and pepper

½ bunch kale, stemmed and chopped (about 8 cups)

1 cup heavy cream

In a soup pot, brown sausage with red pepper flakes. Remove sausage from pot. Add bacon, and fry until crispy. Drain off excess drippings. Add onion and sauté until translucent. Add garlic and sauté 1–2 minutes more. Add chicken stock to deglaze pot. Add potatoes, and return browned sausage to pot. Simmer on medium heat until potatoes are fork-tender.

Season to taste with salt and pepper. Add kale and cover. Cook just until the kale has wilted. Add heavy cream, stir, and remove from heat.

Taco Corn Soup

SERVES 6

I get nostalgic when I make taco corn soup. It's one meal I remember my dad making for supper when we were kids. And in case you wonder, the seasoned salt I use in many recipes is Lawry's.

1 pound ground beef

1 onion, chopped

1 pint (2 cups) frozen corn, thawed

1 (15½-ounce) can black beans, drained

1 (15½-ounce) can Great Northern beans, drained

1 (28-ounce) can diced tomatoes

1 quart (4 cups) tomato juice

1 tablespoon brown sugar

3 tablespoons Taco Seasoning (p. 83)

1 teaspoon chili powder

½ teaspoon seasoned salt

½ teaspoon salt

½ teaspoon pepper

In a soup pot, brown ground beef and onion. Add remaining ingredients and simmer for 20–30 minutes.

For serving

corn chips

2 cups shredded cheddar cheese

1 cup sour cream

Serve with corn chips, shredded cheese, and plenty of sour cream.

Hearty Chili

SERVES 6

This is the first soup I think about making in the fall. Be sure to make Aunt Shirley's Corn Bread (p. 29) to go along with it.

1 pound ground beef

1 onion, chopped

1 bell pepper, chopped

2 garlic cloves, crushed

1 (28-ounce) can diced tomatoes

1 (15½-ounce) can black beans, drained

1 (15½-ounce) can Great Northern beans, drained

1 quart (4 cups) tomato juice

¼ cup strong coffee

1 tablespoon white vinegar

1 tablespoon brown sugar

2 teaspoons chili powder

1 teaspoon salt

½ teaspoon seasoned salt

½ teaspoon black pepper

½ teaspoon ground cumin

¼ teaspoon paprika

¼ teaspoon dried oregano

⅛ teaspoon cayenne pepper

In a soup pot, brown ground beef. Add onion and bell pepper and sauté until soft. Add garlic and sauté 2 minutes more. Add remaining ingredients. Simmer on low heat for at least 1 hour.

Serve with sour cream.

Vegetable Beef Soup

SERVES 6–8

This is a great way to use leftover roast beef. It's also the way to a man's heart—at least my husband's.

1 pound ground beef or leftover roast beef

2 teaspoons Better Than Bouillon beef base

2 cups hot water

1 quart (4 cups) tomato juice

1 (28-ounce) can diced tomatoes

2 cups frozen green beans, thawed

½ cup chopped carrots

4 medium potatoes, cubed

1 medium onion, chopped

2 stalks celery, chopped

2 teaspoons Worcestershire sauce

1½ tablespoon brown sugar

1½ teaspoon salt

1 teaspoon seasoned salt

1 teaspoon chili powder

½ teaspoon pepper

½ teaspoon dried basil

½ teaspoon dried oregano

3 tablespoons cornstarch, dissolved in ¼ cup cold water

Brown ground beef in large soup pot or cut roast beef into pieces and place in pot. Dissolve beef base in hot water. Add broth to pot, along with tomato juice, vegetables, Worcestershire sauce, brown sugar, and seasonings. (Do not add cornstarch.) Simmer for 30–40 minutes until vegetables are tender and flavors are set. Stir in dissolved cornstarch and simmer until thickened.

Old-Fashioned Country Ham Potpie

SERVES 4

If you happen to eat ham for a holiday meal, save the ham bone to make ham potpie. It will comfort your soul.

1 large ham bone

1 cup diced ham

1 cup half-and-half

salt and pepper

Place ham bone in slow cooker and cover with water. Cook on low for 12–18 hours. Strain broth and skim off fat. Transfer broth to a soup pot and add diced ham. Simmer on low while making the dough.

Potpie dough

2 cups unbleached white flour

½ teaspoon salt

1 cup water

Make potpie dough: In small mixing bowl, mix together flour, salt, and water. Add more flour if too sticky. It will be a soft dough. Dust the counter well with flour and roll out dough as thin as possible. With a pizza cutter, cut into 2-inch squares and drop one by one into simmering broth. Cover and simmer 10 minutes. Add half-and-half (do not allow to boil or it will curdle). Season to taste with salt and freshly ground black pepper.

Chicken and Dumpling Soup

SERVES 6

When cold weather hits, this soup appears on our supper table. These soft dumplings, covered in a creamy soup base, will keep everyone coming back for more.

8 chicken thighs

2 tablespoons butter

1 teaspoon seasoned salt

½ teaspoon pepper

1 cup chopped carrots

½ cup chopped celery

1 medium onion, thinly sliced

1 pint (2 cups) frozen peas, thawed

5 cups chicken stock

1 cup half-and-half

½ cup unbleached white flour

½ teaspoon salt

½ teaspoon pepper

Cut chicken thighs into 1-inch pieces. In a soup pot, melt 2 tablespoons butter, add chicken, and sprinkle with seasoned salt and ½ teaspoon pepper. Cook until chicken is no longer pink and starting to brown. Add carrots, celery, and onions. Cook until carrots are tender. Add peas. Pour in chicken stock. In a 2-cup liquid measuring cup, whisk together half-and-half and flour until smooth. Pour half-and-half mixture into soup pot while stirring soup. Add salt and ½ teaspoon additional pepper. Simmer on low.

Dumplings

2 cups unbleached white flour

4 teaspoons baking powder

½ teaspoon baking soda

1½ teaspoon salt

¼ teaspoon pepper

6 tablespoons cold butter, grated

1¼ cup buttermilk

Make dumplings: In a medium mixing bowl, mix together flour, baking powder, baking soda, salt, and pepper. Add grated butter and mix well. Add buttermilk and stir just until dough comes together. Drop tablespoonfuls of dough into simmering soup. (Don't drop more than a tablespoon per dumpling—they will take much longer to cook.) Cover and simmer 10–15 minutes, or until dumplings are firm.

Nourishing Chicken Noodle Soup

This is my go-to soup when anyone in our family is sick. It's important to use bone broth because of the nutrients it adds. I make my bone broth in my electric pressure canner. Simply cover your leftover roasted chicken bones in water and add a little vinegar (which helps leach the minerals from the bones). Cook on high pressure for two hours. Strain and use. This makes a nice gelatinous bone broth.

4 boneless, skinless chicken thighs

2 tablespoons butter

salt and pepper

1½ cup chopped carrots

1 cup chopped celery

½ onion, diced

1 large garlic clove, crushed

8 cups chicken bone broth

8 ounces wide uncooked egg noodles

1 teaspoon dried parsley flakes

1 teaspoon salt

freshly ground pepper

Cut chicken thighs into 1-inch pieces. In a soup pot, melt butter and add chicken. Sprinkle with salt and pepper as desired. Fry until golden brown. Add carrots, celery, and onion and sauté until tender. Add garlic, bone broth, uncooked egg noodles, parsley flakes, and 1 teaspoon salt and simmer for 30 minutes. Season to taste with additional salt and freshly ground pepper.

Chicken Tortilla Soup

SERVES 4

The toppings on this soup make it so delightful. You may find yourself eating handfuls of fried tortilla strips—they are just that good.

2 tablespoons butter

½ teaspoon ground cumin

½ teaspoon chili powder

¼ teaspoon salt

¼ teaspoon pepper

4 boneless, skinless chicken thighs

½ onion, chopped

1 jalapeño pepper, seeded and diced

2 large garlic cloves, crushed

4 cups chicken stock

1 (14½-ounce) can diced tomatoes

1 (15-ounce) can black beans, rinsed and drained

¼ cup tomato paste

½ teaspoon sugar

½ teaspoon chili powder

½ teaspoon salt

freshly ground pepper, as desired

Melt butter in soup pot. Mix together cumin, ½ teaspoon chili powder, ¼ teaspoon salt, and pepper, and sprinkle on both sides of chicken thighs. Fry chicken on medium-high heat, flipping after 3–4 minutes. Fry until golden brown. Remove from pot and shred with two forks. Set aside.

Add onion, jalapeño pepper, and garlic to the soup pot drippings; sauté until soft. Add shredded chicken, chicken stock, tomatoes, beans, tomato paste, sugar, ½ teaspoon additional chili powder, and ½ teaspoon additional salt. Grind in fresh pepper. Simmer 20–30 minutes so flavors can blend.

Toppings

3 tortillas, cut into ½-inch strips

1 cup sour cream

2 cups shredded cheddar cheese

2 avocados, chopped and tossed in lemon juice

½ cup chopped fresh cilantro

While soup is simmering, heat ½ inch oil in a skillet. Add tortilla strips and fry until crispy. Drain on paper towel.

Serve soup hot with tortilla strips and other toppings of your choice.

Creamy White Chili

SERVES 6

This is a hearty and creamy chili with a little kick of spice.

3 boneless, skinless chicken breasts

1 tablespoon canola oil

1 medium onion, chopped

4 garlic cloves, crushed

4 cups chicken stock

2 (15½-ounce) cans Great Northern beans, rinsed and drained

2 (4-ounce) cans green chilies, chopped

1 teaspoon ground cumin

1 teaspoon dried oregano

¼ teaspoon cayenne pepper

1 teaspoon salt

½ teaspoon pepper

1 cup sour cream

½ cup heavy cream

Cut chicken into 1-inch pieces. In a soup pot, heat oil, and add chicken, onion, and garlic. Sauté until chicken is no longer pink. Add chicken stock, beans, chilies, cumin, oregano, cayenne pepper, salt, and pepper. Bring to boil. Reduce heat and simmer for 30 minutes. Remove from heat and stir in sour cream and heavy cream.

Salads, Dressings, Sauces, and Seasonings

I always serve a green salad with our meals. Salads have a way of rounding out meals and adding nutrition and color. I try to always keep one homemade dressing in the refrigerator so it can quickly be used up. Keeping too many dressings on hand at one time can cause confusion about which one is still fresh and can lead to waste.

Homemade sauces and dressings have a way of making foods seem extra special. Imagine dipping hot and crispy Sweet Potato Fries (p. 97) in a tiny bowl of homemade Southwest Dipping Sauce (p. 82). It creates a feeling I just can't explain. Maybe that old saying really is true: the secret is in the sauce!

Fresh Berry Medley

SERVES 8–10

This recipe comes from my sister-in-law, Nadya. I love how light and fresh the lemon zest makes it.

1 cup sparkling wine or white grape juice

½ cup sugar

⅛ teaspoon salt

1½ teaspoon lemon zest

1 tablespoon lemon juice

½ teaspoon vanilla extract

8 cups mixed fresh berries (strawberries, raspberries, and blueberries)

In a small saucepan, combine all ingredients except the fruit. Heat to boiling. Refrigerate until chilled.

In medium bowl, toss fruit with chilled sauce. Refrigerate an additional 1–2 hours before serving. Garnish with fresh mint, if desired.

Festive Cranberry Salad

SERVES 30

This is my grandma Shank's recipe. It makes a lot, so it's a great dish for large family gatherings at Thanksgiving or Christmas. It just wouldn't be Thanksgiving without Grandma's cranberry salad!

1 (12-ounce) bag fresh cranberries

1 cup sugar

1 cup water

3 (3-ounce) boxes raspberry gelatin

2 cups hot water

3 cups cold water

6 apples, grated

4 oranges, cubed

1 (20-ounce) can crushed pineapple (do not drain)

½ cup finely chopped celery

In a small saucepan, cook cranberries, sugar, and 1 cup water until cranberries pop open and mixture thickens slightly.

In a large bowl, dissolve raspberry gelatin in 2 cups hot water. Add 3 cups cold water. Add cooked cranberry mixture and mix well. Refrigerate until the mixture starts to gel (this helps prevent the fruit from soaking up the gelatin color), then fold in apples, oranges, pineapple, and celery.

Refrigerate overnight until gelled.

NOTE: Do not use fresh pineapple! Your gelatin will not gel.

Oil and Vinegar Pasta Salad

SERVES 8

This pasta salad is a great addition to summer picnics. It's also a great way to use fresh garden vegetables. The vegetables listed here are simply a guide; I usually use whatever vegetables I have on hand.

1 12 oz. box or 4 cups uncooked
   tricolor rotini pasta

1 teaspoon salt

2 cups chopped cucumbers

1 cup chopped tomatoes

¼ red onion, chopped

Cook pasta with 1 teaspoon salt according to package directions. Drain.

Dressing

1 cup oil

¾ cup white vinegar

¾ cup sugar

½ teaspoon salt

In a large bowl, whisk together dressing ingredients and add warm pasta. Cover and refrigerate for at least 6 hours. Mix in chopped vegetables 2 hours before serving.

Crunchy Broccoli Salad

SERVES 6–8

This salad is packed with color and flavor. It's a great way to enjoy fresh broccoli from your garden.

6–8 cups chopped
   broccoli

⅔ cup dried cranberries

½ cup chopped spring
   onions

½ cup chopped pecans

Dressing

1 cup mayonnaise

3 tablespoons white
   vinegar

⅓ cup sugar

¼ teaspoon salt

In a medium bowl, toss together broccoli, dried cranberries, spring onions, and pecans. In a 2-cup liquid measuring cup, whisk together dressing ingredients. Pour desired amount of dressing over salad and toss just before serving.

Dad's Favorite Potato Salad

SERVES 10

This recipe comes from my mom. It's one of my dad's favorites. You can bet he will always request it for his birthday meal, along with Pulled Pork Barbecue (p. 144).

2 pounds potatoes

1 tablespoon salt

5 hard-cooked eggs, grated or chopped

½ cup chopped onion

¾ cup diced celery

Peel and halve potatoes and place in a large pot of water. Add salt. Cook just until tender, about 15 minutes. They should pierce easily with a fork but still be firm. Cool quickly in ice water, then grate or dice.

Dressing

1½ cup mayonnaise

2 tablespoons yellow mustard

3 tablespoons white vinegar

½ cup sugar

1½ teaspoon salt

In a medium bowl, whisk together dressing ingredients. Add cooked potatoes, eggs, onion, and celery. Toss well. Refrigerate for 12 hours before serving.

Creamy Coleslaw

SERVES 12

I like a creamy dressing for coleslaw with just enough sweetness and some zip at the end. I often grate a whole head of cabbage in my food processor and mix up the dressing to keep in the refrigerator. Then I have the ingredients on hand so that I can quickly toss together coleslaw for meals all week.

1 head cabbage, grated

1 large carrot, peeled and grated

In a large bowl, toss together cabbage and carrots.

Dressing

½ cup canola oil

½ cup mayonnaise

⅓ cup white vinegar

1 tablespoon yellow mustard

1 small onion, quartered

½ cup sugar

1 teaspoon salt

½ teaspoon celery seed

Blend dressing ingredients well in a blender and refrigerate until ready to toss with cabbage and carrots. Toss desired amount of cabbage mixture with dressing right before serving.

Fresh Garden Salsa

SERVES 4

A fresh-tasting summer snack that goes well with tortilla chips, tacos, enchiladas, burritos, and even eggs.

2 cups diced and drained fresh tomatoes

1 cup blanched fresh corn kernels

½ green bell pepper, diced

⅓ cup diced onion

1 jalapeño pepper, finely chopped

1 teaspoon chopped fresh cilantro

juice of ½ lemon

¼ teaspoon sugar

½ teaspoon salt

⅛ teaspoon pepper

In a medium bowl, mix together ingredients. Refrigerate 1 hour before serving so flavors can blend.

Cold Taco Salad

SERVES 6 – 8

A quick, cool summer meal that tastes great paired with iced mint tea. Taco salad also makes a great packed lunch to take away.

Meat and beans

1 pound ground beef

1 medium onion, chopped

1 (15½-ounce) can black beans, drained

2 tablespoons Taco Seasoning (p. 83)

In a skillet, brown ground beef with onion. Add beans and taco seasoning. Stir. Remove from heat and allow to cool.

Dressing

1 cup mayonnaise

¼ cup ketchup

2 tablespoons white vinegar

1 teaspoon yellow mustard

¼ cup sugar

½ teaspoon paprika

¼ teaspoon salt

In a 2-cup liquid measuring cup, whisk together dressing ingredients.

Salad

1 large head romaine lettuce, chopped

3 tomatoes, chopped

1 large cucumber, sliced

2 cups shredded cheddar cheese

small bag of corn chips, crushed

2 (2¼-ounce) cans sliced black olives

In a large mixing bowl, combine meat mixture, lettuce, tomato, cucumber, cheese, crushed chips, and olives. Toss with enough dressing to coat evenly. Serve immediately.

Chicken Salad

SERVES 4

A quick way to make a tasty lunch with leftover chicken.

½ cup mayonnaise

1 tablespoon honey

2 teaspoons white vinegar

1 teaspoon Dijon mustard

½ teaspoon seasoned salt

½ teaspoon pepper

2 cups chopped cooked chicken

⅓ cup chopped sweet dill pickles

4 hard-cooked eggs, diced

1 stalk celery, chopped

2 tablespoons diced onion

In a medium bowl, mix together mayonnaise, honey, vinegar, and mustard; add seasoned salt and pepper. Fold in chicken, pickles, eggs, celery, and onion. Refrigerate for 30 minutes before serving. Serve on bread, crackers, or lettuce leaves.

Grandma's Pickled Eggs

MAKES 18 EGGS

Grandma used to make pickled eggs every Easter. Now that she's older she can't do that anymore. But I'm so thankful to have her recipe.

18 eggs

Carefully place eggs in a large pot and cover with water. Bring to a hard boil. Remove from heat, cover, and let stand for 12 minutes. Remove eggs from pot and place in a bowl of ice water. Peel and place in a half-gallon jar.

Syrup

1 cup beet juice (drain from 1 pint pickled beets; see instructions)

1 cup white vinegar

1 cup sugar

1 teaspoon salt

If you don't quite have a full cup of beet juice, add water to the beets in the jar and shake it a bit to get more juice. In a small saucepan, mix together beet juice, vinegar, sugar, and salt. Bring to a boil. Pour hot syrup over eggs and refrigerate. Shake the jar a couple of times a day so the eggs are pickled evenly. The eggs are ready to eat after 3 days and will keep up to 1 month.

Ranch Dressing

MAKES ABOUT 1½ CUP

You will find yourself drizzling this dressing over many things. It's that good. We use it to top chicken fajitas, taco salad, and green salads. If you don't have fresh parsley on hand, dried parsley flakes will work.

1 garlic clove, crushed

1 teaspoon chopped fresh parsley

1 cup mayonnaise

½ cup buttermilk

1 teaspoon white vinegar

1 teaspoon lemon juice

1 teaspoon sugar

½ teaspoon salt

½ teaspoon black pepper

⅛ teaspoon cayenne pepper

⅛ teaspoon paprika

In a small bowl, mix together ingredients until well combined. Refrigerate until ready to serve.

Classic Creamy Dressing

MAKES ABOUT 3 CUPS

I use this dressing on cucumber salads, fresh garden salads, thinly sliced cabbage, and watercress. For a different twist you can use lime juice instead of vinegar. The lime juice version pairs well with cabbage.

2 cups mayonnaise

⅓ cup milk

3 tablespoons white vinegar

⅓ cup sugar

½ teaspoon salt

In a small bowl, whisk together ingredients. Serve on the side with a salad or toss right before serving.

Poppy Seed Dressing

MAKES ABOUT 1 CUP

This dressing is delightful drizzled on a leafy lettuce salad garnished with pears or strawberries. If the dressing separates after being chilled, vigorously shake the dressing in a jar with a tightly closed lid. It will emulsify again.

½ cup canola oil	¼ cup chopped onion
3 tablespoons white vinegar	⅓ cup sugar
	½ teaspoon salt
1 teaspoon yellow mustard	½ teaspoon poppy seeds

Place all ingredients except poppy seeds in a blender and blend well. Stir in poppy seeds.

Celery Seed Dressing

MAKES ABOUT 2 CUPS

This recipe has been a part of my family for years! If the dressing separates after being chilled, vigorously shake the dressing in a jar with a tightly closed lid. It will emulsify again.

1 cup canola oil	¼ cup chopped onion
⅓ cup white vinegar	⅔ cup sugar
1½ teaspoon yellow mustard	1 teaspoon salt
	1 teaspoon celery seeds

Place all ingredients in a blender and blend well. Refrigerate until ready to serve.

Balsamic Vinaigrette

MAKES ABOUT 1 CUP

A classic vinaigrette with great flavor. If the dressing separates after being chilled, vigorously shake the dressing in a jar with a tightly closed lid. It will emulsify again.

½ cup olive oil
¼ cup honey
¼ cup balsamic vinegar

1 tablespoon Dijon mustard
⅛ teaspoon salt
freshly ground pepper, to taste

Pour all ingredients into a pint jar and shake well.

vinegar
¼ cup blue cheese crumbles

¼ teaspoon salt
¼ teaspoon pepper

In a small bowl, mix together all ingredients. Refrigerate until ready to serve.

Honey Mustard Dressing

MAKES ABOUT 1½ CUP

This can be used as a salad dressing or a dipping sauce. It's delightful as a dip for Crispy Chicken Nuggets (p. 184).

1 cup mayonnaise

⅓ cup honey

2 tablespoons yellow mustard

1 teaspoon white vinegar

dash paprika

dash salt

In a small bowl, mix together ingredients. Refrigerate until ready to serve.

Tartar Sauce

MAKES ABOUT ½ CUP

Serve this with Baked Fish (p. 198) or Crab Cakes (p. 202).

¼ cup sour cream

¼ cup mayonnaise

1 tablespoon sweet pickle relish

½ teaspoon lemon juice

¼ teaspoon dried dill weed

In a small bowl, mix together ingredients. Refrigerate until ready to serve.

Creamy Horseradish Sauce

MAKES ABOUT 2 CUPS

This sauce is lovely when paired with Traditional Roast Beef (p. 136).

1 cup sour cream

1 cup mayonnaise

¼ cup Dijon mustard

2 tablespoons cream-style horseradish

1 teaspoon lemon juice

1 teaspoon sugar

½ teaspoon salt

In a small bowl, mix together ingredients well.

French Fry Sauce

MAKES ABOUT 2 CUPS

A great dipping sauce for crispy french fries.

1 cup mayonnaise

1 cup ketchup

4 teaspoons white vinegar

½ teaspoon pepper

¼ teaspoon salt

¼ teaspoon paprika

⅛ teaspoon cayenne pepper

In a small bowl, mix together ingredients.

Cocktail Sauce

MAKES ABOUT 1 CUP

An easy homemade cocktail sauce that pairs nicely with Classic Steamed Shrimp (p. 196).

¾ cup ketchup

1 tablespoon lemon juice

½ teaspoon Worcestershire sauce

2 teaspoons horseradish sauce

2 teaspoons brown sugar

¼ teaspoon salt

freshly ground pepper, to taste

In a small bowl, mix together ingredients. Refrigerate until ready to serve.

Southwest Dipping Sauce

MAKES ABOUT 1¼ CUP

This sauce is delightful with Sweet Potato Fries (p. 97).

1 cup mayonnaise

¼ cup ketchup

1 teaspoon white vinegar

¼ teaspoon paprika

dash salt

In a small bowl, mix together ingredients well. Refrigerate until ready to serve.

Taco Seasoning

Once you make your own taco seasoning, you will always make your own! It's my secret ingredient in many taco dishes. One piece of advice: Be sure to buy quality spices. It will make all the difference.

¼ cup chili powder

2 tablespoons ground cumin

4 teaspoons salt

2 teaspoons black pepper

2 teaspoons paprika

1 teaspoon garlic powder

1 teaspoon dried oregano

½ teaspoon red pepper flakes (optional)

Place ingredients in a jar and shake well.

Pork Rub

Using this rub is like rubbing magic on pork. You will soon want to use it on every pork dish you make. It's that good. I use it on ribs, pork chops, pork roast, pork loin . . . am I missing any pork cuts?

3 tablespoons brown sugar

1 tablespoon pepper

1 tablespoon salt

Mix together ingredients, rub on pork, and prepare as usual for the dish you are making. If I remember to do so in time, I put this rub on the pork several hours before cooking so the flavors can mingle. If the pork will sit more than an hour before cooking, be sure to refrigerate it.

Vegetables and Side Dishes

Vegetables are the tools for making a colorful meal. My mom always made sure our meals weren't all the same color. Since we grow most of our vegetables, I don't like to add much to them. For meals, I almost always fix a meat, hot starch, hot vegetable, and green salad. If I am making a richer meat dish (for example, one with gravy or sauce), I don't make a creamy vegetable. Instead I usually prepare a roasted vegetable and a colorful salad. If we are having creamed corn as a hot vegetable, I also try to make sweet potatoes to add a pop of color.

Red-Skinned Mashed Potatoes

SERVES 12

This recipe can also use regular white mashed potatoes. If using Yukon Gold potatoes, add less milk because they contain more moisture. No matter what kind of potatoes you use, don't over-mash them. Mashing them releases starch, and too much mashing can make them gluey.

5 pounds red potatoes, scrubbed and quartered

1 teaspoon salt

½ cup butter, softened

1 (8-ounce) package cream cheese

1 cup sour cream

1 cup milk, warmed

2 teaspoons salt

¼ teaspoon onion powder

Place potatoes into a large pot and cover with water. Add 1 teaspoon salt. Bring to a boil and cook until you can easily poke through them with a fork (20–25 minutes); drain. Place in a mixing bowl and beat with an electric mixer until smooth. Add softened butter and beat until incorporated. Add cream cheese and sour cream, then add warm milk, ¼ cup at a time, until potatoes are creamy but not runny. Add 2 teaspoons salt and onion powder. Mix well and season to taste with additional salt.

Spread into a greased baking dish and cover with foil. Bake at 350°F for 45 minutes until hot and bubbly. Garnish with melted butter and parsley flakes or fresh chives, if desired.

TIP: Unbaked, these potatoes freeze well. When thawed, the texture will seem different, but once they are baked they will be fine.

Brown Butter Potatoes

SERVES 6

This is an old recipe that my grandma says her mother taught her to make. It's a great way to fix new garden potatoes.

3 pounds potatoes, scrubbed and quartered

1 teaspoon salt

½ cup butter

⅔ cup unbleached white flour

¼ cup chopped fresh parsley

½ teaspoon salt

freshly ground pepper

Place potatoes in a large pot and cover with water. Add 1 teaspoon salt. Cook until just tender, or about 20 minutes; drain.

In a large, deep skillet, melt butter. Add flour and stir until smooth and starting to brown. Add chopped parsley and ½ teaspoon salt. Add cooked potatoes, tossing until evenly coated. Sprinkle freshly ground pepper on top and garnish with additional fresh parsley, if desired. Serve with sour cream.

Cheesy Creamed Potatoes

SERVES 6

This recipe is a new take on the classic gourmet potatoes that I grew up eating.

1½ pound potatoes

½ cup chopped onion

2 tablespoons butter

2 tablespoons unbleached white flour

1 cup milk

1 teaspoon salt

½ cup sour cream

1½ cup shredded cheddar cheese, divided

½ teaspoon dried parsley flakes

Peel potatoes and cook until just tender (around 15 minutes). They should pierce easily with a fork but still be firm. Cool quickly in ice water, then grate. This should yield about 4 cups grated potatoes.

In a small skillet, sauté onions in a little oil until translucent. Set aside.

In a saucepan, melt butter; add flour and whisk until smooth. Add milk and salt; cook until thickened. Remove from heat and add sour cream, 1 cup shredded cheddar cheese, and parsley flakes. Fold in grated potatoes and sautéed onions. Spoon into a greased 9-inch cast iron skillet or 9-inch baking dish. Sprinkle remaining ½ cup cheese on top and garnish with additional parsley flakes. Bake, covered, at 350°F for 30 minutes, then uncover and bake 10 minutes more.

Rosemary Roasted Potatoes

SERVES 10

One of my favorite summer meals is grilled chicken, creamed peas, a garden salad, and these potatoes. My aunt Bonnie created this potato recipe for our wedding. It's a favorite of mine—simple yet delicious. I often serve this dish when I have Sunday company.

3 pounds red potatoes

⅓ cup olive oil

1 tablespoon minced fresh rosemary

1 tablespoon minced fresh chives

1 teaspoon salt

1 teaspoon pepper

¼ teaspoon garlic powder

Scrub potatoes and cut into quarters (you will have about 8 cups). In a small bowl, mix together oil and seasonings. In a large bowl, toss oil mixture over potatoes and spread out on a large baking sheet lined with parchment paper. Bake at 425°F for 35 minutes. Serve with sour cream.

Baked Sweet Potatoes

with Cinnamon Butter

SERVES 4 – 6

I'll eat a baked sweet potato any day of the week. I love them. This cinnamon butter adds a special touch.

4 large sweet potatoes
oil
salt and pepper

Clean sweet potatoes well and poke all over with a fork. Rub with oil. Place on a baking sheet lined with parchment paper and bake at 400°F for 45 minutes, or until soft.

Cinnamon butter
½ cup butter, softened
⅓ cup brown sugar
½ teaspoon ground cinnamon
½ teaspoon salt

In a mixing bowl, beat together cinnamon butter ingredients until smooth. Use a small cookie scoop to scoop butter onto a plate. Refrigerate until set.

Slice open baked sweet potatoes and top with a scoop or two of cinnamon butter. Season to taste with salt and pepper.

Citrus-Glazed Sweet Potatoes

SERVES 4

The lemon juice makes these potatoes vibrant.

2 large sweet potatoes, peeled and
cut into wedges (about 6 cups)

juice of ½ lemon

2 tablespoons olive oil

3 tablespoons honey

¾ teaspoon salt

½ teaspoon pepper

¼ teaspoon ground cumin

¼ teaspoon garlic powder

⅛ teaspoon cayenne pepper
(optional)

Place sweet potato wedges in a 9 x 13-inch baking dish lined with parchment paper. In a small bowl, mix together remaining ingredients. Drizzle glaze over potatoes and toss with hands until evenly coated. Bake at 425°F for 30 minutes, stirring halfway through.

Maple-Glazed Sweet Potatoes

SERVES 4 – 6

This is a simple way to make a tasty side dish. It's a twist on the classic candied sweet potatoes made at Thanksgiving.

2 large sweet potatoes

2–3 tablespoons olive oil

maple syrup

salt

Peel sweet potatoes and slice into ¾-inch rounds. Place in a bowl and coat evenly with oil. Lay on a baking sheet lined with parchment paper. Drizzle tops with maple syrup and sprinkle with salt. Bake at 400°F for 30–35 minutes. Flip potatoes halfway through the baking time. This helps coat both sides in the maple syrup. The potatoes are done when they are soft but not falling apart.

Parmesan Roasted Sweet Potatoes

SERVES 4

There is something special about tiny cubes of sweet potatoes. Maybe it's because you know someone took the time to cut them, and you can feel the love that's been poured into them. For a colorful twist, substitute half the sweet potatoes with white potatoes.

3 medium sweet potatoes, peeled and cubed (about 5 cups)

1 large garlic clove, minced or crushed

2 tablespoons butter, melted

1 tablespoon olive oil

½ teaspoon salt

¼ cup freshly grated Parmesan cheese

Place potatoes in a 9 x 13-inch baking dish lined with parchment paper. In a small bowl, mix together garlic, melted butter, oil, and salt. Drizzle butter mixture over potatoes and toss with hands until evenly coated. Sprinkle cheese on top. Bake at 425°F for 20 minutes, or until potatoes are soft and slightly brown. Garnish with parsley flakes and freshly ground pepper, if desired. Add more salt to taste if needed.

Sweet Potato Fries

SERVES 4

It's amazing how many sweet potatoes you can eat when they are cut into fries! The cornstarch in this recipe makes them crispier.

4 large sweet potatoes (about 2 pounds), peeled and cut into ½-inch fries

2 tablespoons canola oil

1 tablespoon cornstarch

1 teaspoon seasoned salt

1 teaspoon garlic powder

1 teaspoon salt

½ teaspoon pepper

¼ teaspoon ground cumin

⅛ teaspoon cayenne pepper (optional)

Place fries in a gallon-sized resealable plastic bag. Add canola oil, close bag, and flip bag over and over until fries are evenly coated in oil.

In a small bowl, mix together remaining ingredients and sprinkle into bag. Repeat flipping process until fries are evenly coated with seasoning mixture. Evenly space fries on two baking sheets lined with parchment paper. (Make sure fries aren't touching. If they are too close together, they will steam instead of roast, resulting in soggy fries.) Bake at 425°F for 30 minutes, flipping the fries halfway through. Baking times may vary; bake until the fries are soft on the inside and crispy on the outside. Serve with Southwest Dipping Sauce (p. 82).

Creamy Macaroni and Cheese

SERVES 6

I've made this recipe for years. Making a white sauce with milk gives this macaroni a wonderful texture. If you are a processed cheese fan, go ahead and use it! You may just need to cut back on the salt.

2 cups uncooked elbow macaroni

1 tablespoon butter

½ teaspoon salt

In a medium saucepan, boil macaroni with butter and salt, or according to package directions, until just done (about 8 minutes). Drain and set aside.

White sauce

¼ cup butter

2 tablespoons unbleached white flour

3 cups milk

1 teaspoon Dijon mustard

1 heaping teaspoon salt

½ teaspoon pepper

1 cup shredded mild cheddar cheese

1 cup shredded Monterey Jack or Gouda cheese

½ cup additional shredded cheese

Make white sauce: In a saucepan on low heat, melt butter and then add flour, whisking until smooth. Cook 1 minute. Add milk, Dijon mustard, salt, and pepper. Heat on low until slightly thickened. Do not boil. Remove from heat and add cheddar and Monterey Jack cheese. Stir until melted.

Stir macaroni into sauce and then pour into a greased baking dish. (I like to use my 10-inch cast iron skillet, but a 9 x 13-inch dish also works.) Sprinkle ½ cup shredded cheese on top. Bake at 350°F for 15–20 minutes until bubbling hot and the cheese on top melts. The sauce should thicken but remain creamy; it will set further as it cools on the table.

Slow-Baked Macaroni

SERVES 6

A quick side dish for Sunday lunch that can be ready the moment you walk in the door from church.

2 cups uncooked elbow macaroni

2 tablespoons butter, melted

2 teaspoons salt

2 cups shredded cheese (I use Gouda and cheddar)

4½ cups milk

In a 9 x 13-inch baking dish, mix together macaroni, melted butter, and salt. Add cheese and mix until evenly combined. Pour milk over top. Bake, covered, at 235°F for 3 hours.

Oven-Roasted Green Beans

SERVES 4

Roasting green beans in the oven enhances their flavor. I used to can all my green beans, but now I freeze them all and roast them in the oven. The texture and color surpass canned green beans.

1 quart (4 cups) frozen green beans, thawed

1 teaspoon salt

¼ cup water

1 small onion, sliced

3 slices bacon

2 teaspoons brown sugar

Place green beans in a buttered 9 x 9-inch baking dish or cast iron skillet. Sprinkle salt on top and toss with hands to coat evenly. Add a small amount of water to help keep the beans moist while roasting. Sprinkle onions over beans. With kitchen scissors, snip bacon pieces evenly over top. Sprinkle with brown sugar. Bake at 375°F for 45 minutes.

TIP: If using canned green beans, use only ¼ teaspoon salt and bake for 30 minutes.

Honey Green Beans

SERVES 4

I've made these green beans for weddings and banquets. It's a different twist on the classic green bean. The honey makes them special.

2 tablespoons bacon grease or butter

¼ onion, sliced

4 cups frozen, uncut green beans

2 tablespoons honey

1 teaspoon salt

In a large skillet, melt bacon grease and add onions. Sauté until translucent. Add green beans; drizzle with honey and sprinkle with salt. Cover and cook 10 minutes, or until beans are just slightly crunchy. Uncover and simmer on high for a few minutes to reduce the liquid in the pan.

Grilled Mushrooms

A great summer side dish when you are grilling. I prefer these over candy—they are that good!

1 pound fresh mushrooms
¼ cup butter
2 garlic cloves, crushed
½ teaspoon salt
½ teaspoon pepper
½ teaspoon dried parsley flakes

Use a dry brush to clean mushrooms. (Do not wash or they will get soggy.) Cut large mushrooms in half and leave medium and small mushrooms whole.

In a small saucepan, melt butter; add garlic, salt, pepper, and parsley flakes. About 30 minutes before grilling, pour butter mixture over mushrooms and toss. Place on hot grill and grill until tender.

Classic Bread Stuffing

SERVES 6

This stuffing is sure to become a regular addition to your Thanksgiving feast.

12 slices sandwich bread, toasted
¼ cup butter
½ medium onion, diced
1 cup chopped carrots
2 stalks celery, diced
2 cups chicken stock
1 teaspoon salt
½ teaspoon pepper
½ teaspoon poultry seasoning
3 eggs
1 cup milk

Tear toasted bread into pieces and place in a 9 x 13-inch baking dish.

In a saucepan, melt butter and sauté onion until translucent. Add carrots, celery, chicken stock, salt, pepper, and poultry seasoning, and simmer until carrots are tender. Remove from heat.

In a small bowl, beat together eggs and milk. Slowly pour egg mixture into broth mixture, stirring quickly so the eggs don't cook and make clumps. Pour mixture over bread pieces. Bake at 350°F for 35 minutes.

Creamed Lima Beans (or Peas)

SERVES 4

Add these to a meal of grilled pork chops and roasted sweet potatoes and you will be happy.

1 pint (2 cups) frozen lima beans, thawed

2 tablespoons water

1 tablespoon butter

1 teaspoon sugar

½ teaspoon salt

½ cup half-and-half

2 teaspoons cornstarch

In a saucepan, stir together lima beans, water, butter, sugar, and salt. Cover and simmer until tender but not soft (about 8 minutes). In a 1-cup liquid measuring cup, whisk together half-and-half and cornstarch. Stir mixture into beans, and keep stirring until thickened. Remove from heat. If the creamed lima beans are too thick, stir in a little more half-and-half.

TIP: This is the same creaming method I use for peas. If buying peas, make sure they are labeled baby or petite peas. Cook peas 2 minutes before adding thickening. If they are too thick, stir in a little more half-and-half. Don't overcook or peas will get chalky.

Roasted Broccoli

SERVES 4

A flavorful and easy way to prepare fresh broccoli. Don't worry if there are dark brown tips after roasting—they are full of flavor.

6 cups fresh broccoli spears

2 tablespoons olive oil

1 garlic clove, crushed

salt and pepper

Line a baking sheet with parchment paper. In a bowl, toss together broccoli, oil, and garlic. Distribute broccoli evenly on the baking sheet and sprinkle salt and pepper on top. Bake at 475°F for 15 minutes.

Perfect Broccoli

SERVES 4

Something about adding the sugar to the water makes this cooked broccoli method hard to beat.

½ cup water

1 teaspoon sugar

4 cups chopped frozen or fresh broccoli

salt

Combine water and sugar in a large saucepan. Bring to a boil; add broccoli. Cover and cook 5–8 minutes, or until just tender. Sprinkle with salt and serve immediately.

Rice and Beans

SERVES 4

I use this as a side for many of my main dishes. I like to use basmati rice for this recipe.

1 tablespoon oil

1½ cup uncooked rice, rinsed

1 teaspoon salt

1 tablespoon cream of coconut (optional)

1 (15½-ounce) can black beans, drained

2 cups water

Heat oil in a pot; add rice, salt, and cream of coconut, if desired. Cook and stir rice until it is slightly toasted (toasting rice adds flavor). Add black beans and water. Stir well. Cover and bring to a hard boil; turn to lowest heat and cook, covered, for 20 minutes. Remove from heat and let stand for 10 minutes. Fluff with a fork before serving.

TIP: Cream of coconut can usually be found in the mixed drink section of the grocery store.

Stuffed Peppers

SERVES 12

I plant bell peppers in my garden each year just so I can make this recipe. I grew up eating stuffed peppers all summer long. In the summer we would eat fresh tomato sandwiches, corn on the cob, and stuffed peppers for supper.

4–6 large bell peppers (any color)

1 cup crushed crackers

2 cups shredded cheddar cheese

1 cup mayonnaise

2 teaspoons white vinegar

2 teaspoons sugar

¼ teaspoon seasoned salt

¼ teaspoon pepper

Halve (or quarter) and seed bell peppers. In a medium-sized bowl, mix together remaining ingredients. Fill bell pepper halves with mixture. If making ahead of time, wait to add crackers so the filling won't be soggy.

Beef and Pork

We usually have a freezer full of locally raised beef and pork. For beef, we have found that purchasing a whole cow from a farm and then having it processed at a local butcher costs less than buying beef at the grocery store. Not only is it more economical; it tastes better too! For pork, we butcher a pig every year with my family. We vacuum-pack all the meat, and it stays fresh for a long time.

Buying in bulk and butchering may not work for everyone, because you need to have freezer space available, but these methods have worked well for us.

Classic Meat Loaf

with Caramelized Topping

SERVES 4 – 6

This is my go-to ground beef recipe when I need a quick meat dish. The caramelized topping finishes off this meat loaf perfectly.

1 tablespoon butter
1 onion, chopped
½ cup ketchup
1 egg, beaten
1 tablespoon white vinegar
1 tablespoon cornmeal
1 tablespoon brown sugar
1 teaspoon salt
½ teaspoon pepper
1 cup cracker crumbs
1 pound ground beef

In a small skillet, melt butter and sauté onion until starting to brown. Set aside to cool.

In a medium bowl, mix together ketchup, egg, vinegar, cornmeal, brown sugar, salt, and pepper. Stir well. Fold in sautéed onions, cracker crumbs, and ground beef, and mix just until combined. Overmixing can cause a tough and dense meat loaf. Line a baking sheet with parchment paper and form mixture into a 4 x 9-inch loaf. Bake at 350°F for 35 minutes, or until internal temperature reaches 160°F.

Topping
⅓ cup ketchup
1 tablespoon brown sugar
2 teaspoons yellow mustard
several drops liquid smoke

Make topping: Stir together ingredients in a small bowl. Spread over top of cooked meat loaf. Broil at 400°F for 10 minutes, or until top caramelizes. Let stand 10 minutes before cutting so that meat loaf stays together.

Beef Stroganoff

SERVES 4

I grew up eating stroganoff made with ground beef. This is a quick meal that your family will love, especially if you serve it with Honey Green Beans (p. 103) and lettuce salad.

1 pound ground beef

½ onion, chopped

3 garlic cloves, crushed or minced

8 ounces fresh mushrooms, sliced, or 2 (4-ounce) cans sliced mushrooms, drained

2 cups milk

3 tablespoons unbleached white flour

1¼ teaspoon salt

½ teaspoon pepper

¼ teaspoon paprika

½ cup sour cream

12 ounces uncooked egg noodles

½ teaspoon salt

In a large skillet, brown ground beef with onion. Add garlic and mushrooms. Cook until mushrooms are tender.

In a bowl, whisk together milk, flour, 1¼ teaspoon salt, pepper, and paprika. Add to skillet and simmer until thickened. Stir in sour cream and simmer on low heat until heated through.

Cook egg noodles with ½ teaspoon salt according to package directions. Drain.

Serve stroganoff on a bed of egg noodles. Garnish with parsley, if desired.

Taco Salad

If I call Joshua while he's at work and ask him what to make for supper, he almost always requests taco salad.

1 pound ground beef

½ onion, chopped

1 (15½-ounce) can black beans, drained

1 (6-ounce) can tomato paste

1 quart (4 cups) tomato juice

2 tablespoons Taco Seasoning (p. 83)

2 tablespoons brown sugar

¼ teaspoon salt

¼ teaspoon red pepper flakes

corn chips, crushed

Toppings

shredded cheese

chopped lettuce

chopped tomatoes

chopped onions

sliced black olives

Ranch Dressing (p. 77)

In a pot, brown ground beef with onions. Add remaining ingredients except for corn chips and simmer for 30 minutes.

Serve on a bed of crushed corn chips with toppings. Drizzle with dressing.

Spaghetti

with Flavorful Meat Sauce

SERVES 6 – 8

I like to mix ground beef and pork for my spaghetti sauce. Adding the cream at the end creates a lovely mellow tomato flavor that keeps you coming back for more. This is a large recipe; sometimes I freeze half the meat sauce and only cook half the spaghetti. Serve with Perfect Broccoli (p. 108) and a salad.

1 pound uncooked spaghetti

1 pound ground beef

1 pound ground pork sausage

1 medium onion, diced

4 garlic cloves, crushed

1 (6-ounce) can tomato paste

2 quarts (8 cups) tomato juice

¼ cup white wine

2 teaspoons brown sugar

1 tablespoon dried basil

2 teaspoons dried parsley

1 teaspoon salt

¼ teaspoon black pepper

¼ teaspoon red pepper flakes

2 tablespoons cornstarch, dissolved in ¼ cup cold water

1 cup half-and-half

Cook spaghetti in salted water until al dente according to package directions. Drain.

In a pot, brown ground beef, sausage, and onion. Add garlic, tomato paste, tomato juice, wine, brown sugar, basil, parsley, salt, pepper, and red pepper flakes and simmer on low for 30 minutes. Add cornstarch mixture and cook until thickened. Stir in half-and-half; add al dente spaghetti and simmer on low 5 minutes more, or until spaghetti is done. Serve with freshly grated Parmesan cheese.

Easy Lasagna

SERVES 10

A timeless recipe from Mom that's easy to assemble. You don't even need to precook your lasagna noodles before assembling. Serve with broccoli and salad.

9–12 uncooked lasagna noodles

Sauce

1 pound ground beef

1 onion, diced

2 garlic cloves, crushed

1 (6-ounce) can tomato paste

1 quart (4 cups) tomato juice

1½ cup water

2 tablespoons brown sugar

1 teaspoon dried oregano

1 teaspoon dried basil

1¼ teaspoon salt

½ teaspoon pepper

Make sauce: In a pot, brown ground beef with onion. Add remaining ingredients. Simmer on low for 15 minutes. (The sauce will seem runny, but the uncooked lasagna noodles will soak up the liquid while baking.)

Cheese filling and topping

16 ounces cottage cheese or ricotta cheese

1 egg, beaten

1 teaspoon dried parsley flakes

½ cup freshly grated Parmesan cheese, divided

2 cups shredded mozzarella cheese

In another bowl, mix together cottage cheese, egg, and parsley flakes.

Place 3–4 noodles in an ungreased 9 x 13-inch baking dish. Top with a third of the meat sauce (about 2½ cups), then half the cottage cheese mixture, then half the Parmesan cheese. Repeat layers one more time. Top with remaining 3–4 noodles and then with remaining meat sauce.

Bake, covered, at 325°F for 45 minutes. Remove cover and sprinkle with mozzarella cheese. Bake, uncovered, for an additional 15 minutes. Garnish with fresh basil, if desired.

Stromboli

SERVES 4 – 6

As kids, my sisters and I could always choose our birthday supper menu, and stromboli was always a favorite. We grew up eating the so-called Mennonite version—with yellow mustard, ham, salami, sausage, and American and mozzarella cheese. You can easily substitute cheddar for the American cheese. This recipe makes nice calzones as well.

Dough

1 cup warm water

1 tablespoon active dry yeast

1 tablespoon olive oil

1 tablespoon honey

2½ cups unbleached white flour

1 teaspoon salt

Traditional filling

6–8 slices hard salami

1 pound ground pork sausage, browned

10 fresh mushrooms, sliced

½ onion, thinly sliced

1 (4-ounce) can sliced black olives

1 jalapeño pepper, thinly sliced

2 cups shredded mozzarella cheese

½ cup freshly grated Parmesan cheese

freshly ground pepper, as desired

Mennonite filling

3 tablespoons yellow mustard

½ pound sliced ham

6 slices salami

¾ pound ground sausage, browned

6 slices American cheese

2 cups shredded mozzarella cheese

freshly ground pepper, as desired

Additional ingredients

1 egg, beaten

1 tablespoon water

dried oregano

marinara sauce, for dipping

Make dough: In a 2-cup liquid measuring cup, whisk together warm water, yeast, oil, and honey. In a medium bowl, combine flour and salt. Make a well in the middle of the flour mixture and pour in yeast mixture. Mix together with a fork until combined. Knead lightly and form into a smooth ball. Cover and let rise 20 minutes.

Sprinkle flour on counter. Knead the dough a little and sprinkle top with flour. Roll into a 12 x 20-inch rectangle. Layer either traditional or Mennonite filling ingredients down the center, in order listed. Fold one side of dough over the filling and wet the top edges with water. Fold the other side of the dough over top and seal ends, pinching tight. Carefully transfer to a greased baking sheet.

Prepare egg wash: Mix together egg and water. Brush top of stromboli with egg wash and sprinkle with dried oregano. Bake at 400°F for 20 minutes. Cover with foil for a few minutes after baking to soften the crust. Slice, and serve with marinara sauce.

To make stromboli ahead of time, assemble and freeze before baking. Thaw completely and let rise before baking—around 2 hours.

TIP: To make calzones, divide risen dough into 4 sections. Roll out into circles and top half the circle with pizza sauce and toppings. Brush edges with egg wash, fold in half, and pinch edges shut. Place on greased baking sheet. Brush tops with egg wash and bake at 400°F for 15 minutes.

Friday Night Pizza

SERVES 4

Joshua loves pizza. He asks if we can eat it every Friday night. This dough is the same as the dough for Cheesy Breadsticks (p. 41) but is refrigerated for 2–3 days to create a chewy texture. See recipe tip below.

Dough

1 cup warm water

1 tablespoon active dry yeast

1 tablespoon olive oil

1 tablespoon honey

2½ cups unbleached white flour

1 teaspoon salt

In a 2-cup liquid measuring cup, whisk together warm water, yeast, oil, and honey. In a medium bowl, combine flour and salt. Make a well in the middle of the flour and pour in the yeast mixture. Mix together with a fork until combined. Knead lightly by hand and form into a smooth ball. Place in a greased bowl, cover, let and rise for at least 1–2 hours.

Toppings

1 cup pizza sauce

2 cups shredded mozzarella cheese

1 cup fried sausage

5 slices bacon, fried and chopped

½ green or red bell pepper, sliced

1 small onion, sliced in rings

1 (2¼-ounce) can sliced black olives

fresh basil, chopped

freshly ground black pepper, as desired

freshly grated Parmesan cheese

Line a baking sheet with parchment paper and lightly grease with oil. Oil your hands and spread out dough 1 inch away from the sides of the baking sheet. (It also works great to use a 14-inch round pizza pan; oil well and dust with cornmeal.) Spread dough with toppings in order listed. Bake at 475°F for 10–12 minutes.

TIP: For a chewier pizza crust, refrigerate dough in an airtight container for 2–3 days. Remove from the refrigerator and let rise 2 hours before baking.

Barbecued Meatballs

SERVES 14

A classic meatball recipe topped with a flavorful sauce. I love this large recipe, which makes about 30 meatballs, because I can put one dish in the freezer to pull out on a busy day.

Meatballs

½ cup diced onion

1 cup milk

2 eggs

2 garlic cloves, crushed, or
   ½ teaspoon garlic powder

2 teaspoons chili powder

2 teaspoons salt

½ teaspoon pepper

3 pounds ground beef

1 cup rolled oats

1 cup cracker crumbs

Make meatballs: In a small skillet, sauté onion in a little oil until translucent. Set aside.

In a large bowl, mix together milk, eggs, garlic, chili powder, salt, and pepper. Fold in ground beef, rolled oats, cracker crumbs, and sautéed onion. Mix just until combined. Form into meatballs using ¼ cup mixture per meatball. Place in a baking dish.

Barbecue sauce

2 cups ketchup

⅔ cup brown sugar

1 garlic clove, crushed, or ½ teaspoon
   garlic powder

½ teaspoon liquid smoke

2 teaspoons lemon juice

pinch cayenne pepper

Make sauce: In a small bowl, mix together sauce ingredients. Top each meatball with a spoonful of sauce.

Bake at 350°F for 45 minutes, or until internal temperature reaches 160°F. Garnish with parsley flakes, if desired.

Savory Meatballs

SERVES 14

I created this recipe, which also makes 30 meatballs, to have another meatball variation. This creamy sauce is full of flavor—I love the combination of the half-and-half, cheeses, and Dijon mustard.

Meatballs

½ cup diced onion

1 cup milk

2 eggs

2 garlic cloves, crushed, or
 ½ teaspoon garlic powder

2 teaspoons chili powder

2 teaspoons salt

½ teaspoon pepper

3 pounds ground beef

1 cup rolled oats

1 cup cracker crumbs

Make meatballs: In a small skillet, sauté onion in a little oil until translucent. Set aside. In a large bowl, mix together milk, eggs, garlic, chili powder, salt, and pepper. Fold in ground beef, rolled oats, cracker crumbs, and onion. Mix just until combined. Form into meatballs using ¼ cup mixture per meatball. Place in a baking dish.

Sauce

2 cups half-and-half

4 ounces cream cheese, cubed

1 tablespoon Dijon mustard

2 cups shredded sharp cheddar
 cheese

1 teaspoon salt

½ teaspoon pepper

¼ teaspoon garlic powder

Make sauce: In a small saucepan, bring half-and-half to a simmer. Add cream cheese and whisk until smooth. Add mustard, cheddar cheese, salt, pepper, and garlic powder. Stir until cheese is melted. Spoon on top of meatballs.

Bake at 350°F for 45 minutes, or until internal temperature reaches 160°F. Garnish with parsley flakes, if desired.

"Poor Man's" Steak

This is one dish I learned to make for Joshua after we were married. He grew up eating "poor man's" steak, but I didn't. The creamy mushroom gravy pairs wonderfully with ground beef. Serve with mashed potatoes because the extra gravy needs a home.

1 egg

¼ teaspoon Worcestershire sauce

1 dash liquid smoke

½ teaspoon salt

¼ teaspoon pepper

½ cup cracker crumbs

¼ cup minced onion

1 pound ground beef

2 tablespoons butter

8 ounces fresh mushrooms, sliced thick, or 2 (4-ounce) cans sliced mushrooms, drained

2 garlic cloves, crushed

In a medium bowl, mix together egg, Worcestershire sauce, liquid smoke, salt, pepper, cracker crumbs, and onion. Fold in ground beef and mix until just combined. Form into 7 round patties using ⅓ cup mixture per patty.

In a large skillet, melt butter, and add patties. Cook on medium heat until both sides are brown. Remove patties from skillet.

Add mushrooms and garlic to pan drippings. Fry until garlic is soft and mushrooms are tender.

Gravy

2 cups milk

2 tablespoons unbleached white flour

½ teaspoon salt

freshly ground pepper, to taste

¼ cup sour cream

Make gravy: In a liquid measuring pitcher, whisk together milk, flour, salt, and pepper. While stirring, add milk mixture to mushrooms in skillet. Simmer until thickened. Add sour cream and stir until smooth. Return patties to skillet and simmer on low for 5 minutes.

Cheesy Beef Enchiladas

SERVES 4 – 6

We love these beef enchiladas. Who doesn't love cheese sauce? Serve with toppings of your choice. I use sour cream, chopped tomatoes, and chopped lettuce. Add Rice and Beans (p. 135) as a side and you have a full meal.

1 pound ground beef

1 onion, chopped

1 tablespoon Taco Seasoning (p. 83)

12 (8-inch) flour tortillas

In a skillet, brown ground beef with onions. Add taco seasoning and stir well.

Fill each tortilla with ¼ cup of meat and roll up. Place seam side down in a greased 9 x 13-inch baking dish.

Cheese sauce

½ cup butter

2 tablespoons unbleached white flour

2 cups milk

1 cup shredded Monterey Jack or cheddar cheese

¼ teaspoon salt

freshly ground black pepper, to taste

Make sauce: In a saucepan, melt butter and add flour, stirring until smooth. Cook for 1 minute. Add milk, cheese, salt, and pepper. Simmer on very low until thickened. Do not boil. Pour over tortillas and bake, covered, at 350°F for 25 minutes, or until bubbly.

Traditional Roast Beef

SERVES 6

A Sunday lunch favorite. I use chicken stock instead of water because it makes a strong, flavorful broth. You can use the broth to cook noodles or to make a delicious gravy. Sometimes I fold chunks of beef into my noodles after they are cooked.

1 (3-pound) chuck roast
salt and pepper
olive oil
1 tablespoon brown sugar
⅓ cup white or red wine
1 bay leaf
4 cups chicken stock

Season all sides of a nice chuck roast with salt and pepper. Add a little oil to a skillet and sear roast on all sides until medium brown (searing adds lots of flavor). Place in a slow cooker. Add brown sugar, wine, and bay leaf, then pour chicken stock over all. Cook on low for 8 hours. Remove roast from broth and plate it. Strain broth, dip off fat, and use broth for gravy or cooking noodles.

NOTE: If serving this for Sunday lunch, cook this in the crockpot the night before. Leave the crockpot on warm while you are at church.

Sliced Beef

SERVES 10–12

An elegant meat for special occasions. Serve with Creamy Horseradish Sauce (p. 81), which is so delightful paired with the sliced beef.

1 (5- to 6-pound) sirloin tip roast

oil

Rub

3 large garlic cloves, crushed

3 tablespoons brown sugar

1 tablespoon salt

1 tablespoon pepper

In a small bowl, mix together rub ingredients and rub on roast. Refrigerate for 3 hours.

In a large skillet, heat some oil and sear roast on all sides until medium brown.

Place in a roasting pan and roast, uncovered, at 300°F until center reaches 145°F (around 2–3 hours). Remove from oven and cover with foil. Let rest 30 minutes. Thinly slice roast just before serving and serve with Creamy Horseradish Sauce (p. 81).

Steak and Cheese Subs

SERVES 6

A flavor-filled "man sandwich" that's fun to make and eat.

Vegetables

2 tablespoons butter

1 green bell pepper, sliced

½ onion, sliced

salt and pepper, as desired

Prepare vegetables: In a skillet, melt 2 tablespoons butter. Add bell pepper and onion and sprinkle with salt and pepper. Sauté until tender. Remove from skillet.

Meat

2 tablespoons butter

2 pounds sirloin steak, cut into ½-inch strips

1 tablespoon Worcestershire sauce

Montreal steak seasoning, as desired

salt and pepper, as desired

Prepare steak: In the same skillet, melt 2 tablespoons additional butter and add steak and Worcestershire sauce. Sprinkle steak seasoning and salt and pepper on top. Cook on high, stirring often. Once the steak starts to brown slightly, return the sautéed vegetables to the skillet and cook a few minutes more. Do not overcook. You want the steak to be pink in the middle, as this makes a juicy sandwich.

Sandwiches

6 hoagie rolls

butter, for spreading

mayonnaise, for spreading

12 slices Muenster cheese

Assemble sandwiches: Cut open hoagie rolls and lay on baking sheet. Spread rolls lightly with butter. Broil in oven until toasted. Remove from oven and spread mayonnaise on the bottom of each roll, then add the steak filling. Top with cheese. Return to oven and broil until cheese is melted. Serve immediately. Use the leftover pan juices for a dipping sauce.

Roasted Pork Loin

SERVES 6

I think the trick to a good pork loin is roasting it slow and not overcooking it. A meat thermometer is a must when roasting pork.

1 (3- to 4-pound) boneless pork loin

Rub
3 tablespoons brown sugar
1 tablespoon salt
1 tablespoon pepper

In a small bowl, mix together rub ingredients and rub all over pork loin. Refrigerate for 2 hours before roasting.

Place pork loin in a roasting pan and roast, uncovered, at 300°F until center reaches 145°F (about 1½ hour).

Remove from oven and cover. Let rest 20 minutes (do not skip this step!) and then slice thin before serving. Serve with barbecue sauce on the side.

Pulled Pork Barbecue

SERVES 6-8

This is an effortless way to make pulled pork. This recipe works with most pork roast cuts, but I prefer a Boston butt. If you are in a hurry, use store-bought sauce instead of homemade. You can also cook any cut of pork roast this way and make a gravy with the broth.

1 (3- to 4-pound) pork Boston butt

olive oil

Rub

3 tablespoons brown sugar

1 tablespoon salt

1 tablespoon pepper

In a small bowl, mix together rub ingredients and rub all over the pork. Heat a little olive oil in a pot and sear pork on all sides until brown. Place in a slow cooker and cook on low for 8 hours.

Barbecue sauce

1 tablespoon butter

½ cup sliced onion

¾ cup ketchup

⅓ cup white vinegar

½ cup water

1 tablespoon Worcestershire sauce

2 teaspoons lemon juice

¼ teaspoon liquid smoke

3 tablespoons brown sugar

2 teaspoons dry mustard

½ teaspoon salt

½ teaspoon pepper

Prepare sauce: In a saucepan, melt butter and add onions. Sauté onions until translucent. Add remaining ingredients and simmer on low for 10 minutes.

After the pork is done, place it on a plate and pull it apart with two forks. Add to the barbecue sauce and simmer for a few minutes. Serve on Pretzel Buns (p. 38) with Creamy Coleslaw (p. 70).

Grilled Pork Chops

SERVES 4 – 6

An elegant meat for guests that is easy to prepare.

8 pork chops
¼ cup butter, melted

Rub

3 tablespoons brown sugar

1 tablespoon salt

1 tablespoon pepper

In a small bowl, mix together rub ingredients and sprinkle all over pork chops. Refrigerate 2–4 hours before grilling.

Place pork chops on a hot grill and brush each side with melted butter while grilling. Grill until insides are no longer pink, or until internal temperature just reaches 145°F. Do not overcook. Serve with barbecue sauce on the side.

Country Fried Pork Chops

SERVES 4 – 6

This recipe is southern comfort food. Serve with fluffy mashed potatoes, and your dining companions will even wash the dishes.

8 boneless pork chops

1 cup unbleached white flour

3 tablespoons butter

seasoned salt

salt and pepper

Dredge pork chops in 1 cup flour. Melt butter in skillet and add pork chops. Sprinkle the first side with seasoned salt and the other side with salt and pepper. Fry until done, or until centers reach 145°F. Remove from skillet, reserving drippings.

Gravy

1 cup half-and-half

1 cup milk

2 tablespoons unbleached white flour

Prepare gravy: Whisk together half-and-half, milk, and 2 tablespoons flour. Add to pan drippings. Simmer until thickened. Taste gravy and add more salt and pepper if desired. Return the pork chops to the skillet with the gravy and simmer on low for a few minutes.

Pork Chops

with Mustard Sauce

SERVES 4 – 6

This recipe offers an elegant way to dress up pork chops. The tangy mustard sauce is great paired with a side of baked sweet potatoes.

8 boneless pork chops

3 tablespoons butter

Rub

3 tablespoons brown sugar

1 tablespoon salt

1 tablespoon pepper

In a small bowl, mix together rub ingredients and rub on pork chops. Refrigerate 2 hours before frying.

In a skillet, melt 3 tablespoons butter and sear pork chops 2 minutes per side, or until centers reach 145°F. Place in a baking dish and place in a 200°F oven to keep warm while making the sauce.

Mustard sauce

1 tablespoon butter

1 garlic clove, crushed

3 tablespoons white wine

$\frac{2}{3}$ cup half-and-half

2 tablespoons Dijon mustard

2 teaspoons lemon juice

Prepare sauce: In the skillet with the pan drippings, add 1 tablespoon butter and sauté garlic until fragrant. Add wine and deglaze the skillet. Add half-and-half and mustard. Simmer until sauce thickens. Remove from heat and add lemon juice. Drizzle over pork chops.

Maple-Glazed Pork Chops

SERVES 4-6

Maple syrup is one of my favorite flavors to pair with pork. The mushrooms add texture and an elegant touch.

8 boneless pork chops

3 tablespoons butter

8 ounces fresh mushrooms, sliced

½ cup chicken stock

⅓ cup maple syrup

Rub

3 tablespoons brown sugar

1 tablespoon salt

1 tablespoon pepper

In a small bowl, mix together rub ingredients and rub on pork chops. Refrigerate 2 hours before frying.

In a skillet, melt butter. Add pork chops and fry until done, 5–6 minutes total, or until internal temperature reaches 145°F. Size and thickness can make a difference in cooking time. When done, remove from skillet.

Add mushrooms to pan drippings. Sauté until tender. Add chicken stock and maple syrup and cook on high until sauce reduces and thickens. Return pork chops to skillet and cook for 1 minute, or until heated through.

Pork Tacos

with Pineapple Salsa

SERVES 8

Pork tacos are my favorite kind of taco. They are so delightful topped with pineapple salsa and sour cream.

2 cups uncooked basmati rice

1 (4- to 5-pound) boneless pork loin

24 (6-inch) flour or corn tortillas

1 (8-ounce) container sour cream

Rub

3 tablespoons brown sugar

1 tablespoon salt

1 tablespoon pepper

1 teaspoon paprika

1 teaspoon dried oregano

½ teaspoon red pepper flakes

Pineapple salsa

1 (20-ounce) can pineapple tidbits, drained well (fresh pineapple works too)

½ jalapeño pepper, minced

½ red onion, diced

¼ cup chopped fresh cilantro

juice of ½ lime

Cook rice according to package directions. In a small bowl, mix together rub ingredients and rub all over pork loin.

In a small bowl, mix together salsa ingredients. Refrigerate so flavors can mingle.

Place pork loin in a roasting pan and roast, covered, at 250°F for 4 hours. Remove from oven and shred with tongs right in the roasting pan. The broth adds wonderful flavor.

Spoon into tortillas and serve with rice, pineapple salsa, and lots of sour cream.

Oven Barbecued Ribs

SERVES 6

I've made this recipe for many of Joshua's birthday suppers. These ribs are stress free in terms of preparation and hard to beat in terms of taste.

1 large rack pork spare ribs (about 5 pounds)

Rub

3 tablespoons brown sugar

1 tablespoon salt

1 tablespoon pepper

Barbecue sauce

1 cup ketchup

2 tablespoons orange juice

¼ teaspoon liquid smoke

¼ cup brown sugar

1 teaspoon dry mustard

¼ teaspoon cayenne pepper

In a small bowl, mix together rub ingredients and rub on ribs. Refrigerate 2 hours before baking.

In a 2-cup liquid measuring cup, mix together sauce ingredients. Reserve ½ cup sauce and set aside.

Place ribs in a large roasting pan and add 1 inch of water. (If you don't have a large roasting pan, a baking sheet covered in foil will work.) Cover and roast at 300°F for 2 hours. Drain off liquid and top with remaining barbecue sauce.

Increase oven temperature to 350°F and bake, covered, 1 hour more. Remove cover and broil at 400°F for 10 minutes until top caramelizes. Cut ribs into serving-sized sections. Place on a large serving platter. Heat reserved sauce and drizzle over ribs before serving.

TIP: The ribs should pull apart easily with a fork but not fall off the bone. If they do not pull apart easily, they need to be roasted longer. Some ribs are thicker than others.

Chicken and Seafood

We really enjoy chicken. I have tried many brands of chicken and have found an antibiotic- and hormone-free brand that I like. I prefer boneless, skinless chicken thighs that come in a tray of eight; it's the perfect amount for our little family. I stock up every couple of weeks and freeze the trays of chicken. They are handy to pull out in the morning and place in the sink or refrigerator to thaw for supper that evening.

We don't eat lots of seafood, but we enjoy it for special occasions. I do make sure to purchase wild-caught seafood. We grew up eating shrimp at Christmas, so it has special memories for me.

Creamy Italian Chicken and Pasta

SERVES 4 – 6

I love to pan-sear meats and make a savory pan sauce with the flavorful drippings. This one is packed with flavor and is pleasing to the eye as well.

Pasta

¾ pound (3 cups) uncooked penne pasta

1 teaspoon salt

1 tablespoon olive oil

Cook pasta with 1 teaspoon salt according to package directions. Drain and coat with olive oil. This helps keep it from sticking together.

Chicken

3 large chicken breasts

salt and pepper

3 tablespoons butter

3 large garlic cloves, crushed

12 grape tomatoes, halved

⅓ cup white wine

1 cup half-and-half

1 cup milk

1 tablespoon cornstarch

1 teaspoon dried parsley flakes

½ teaspoon salt

¼ cup freshly grated Parmesan cheese

With a sharp knife, slice chicken breasts in half lengthwise. Sprinkle both sides with salt and pepper.

In a skillet, melt butter and add chicken. Spread a little crushed garlic on top of each piece of chicken. Fry on medium heat, uncovered, until almost done. Flip and fry other side until golden brown. (Cook 3–4 minutes per side, or until centers reach 165°F.) Remove chicken from skillet.

Add tomatoes to pan drippings, sliced side down. Fry until browned. Remove from skillet and pour in wine. Simmer until it reduces to half. In a liquid measuring cup, whisk together half-and-half, milk, and cornstarch. Pour into wine reduction and simmer until slightly thickened. Add parsley flakes and salt.

Return chicken and tomatoes to the skillet and top with cheese. Cover and simmer for 5 minutes. Serve over pasta. Season to taste with salt.

TIP: A good method for cutting chicken is to place your non-cutting hand flat on top of the chicken breast and apply pressure. Then use your knife to cut down the middle of the breast.

Chicken Parmesan

SERVES 4–6

A classic Italian dish that children and adults will love.

3 large chicken breasts

1 cup buttermilk

¼ cup butter

1 pound uncooked spaghetti

1 teaspoon salt

1 tablespoon olive oil

Breading

1 cup panko bread crumbs

1 cup unbleached white flour

1 teaspoon dried parsley flakes

2 teaspoons salt

¼ teaspoon pepper

In a pie pan, mix together breading ingredients. With a sharp knife, slice chicken breasts in half. Dip chicken in buttermilk, then coat with breading.

In a large skillet, melt butter. Add chicken. Fry on medium heat, uncovered, until mostly done. Flip and fry other side until golden brown. Remove chicken from skillet and place in a 9 x 13-inch baking dish. (If frying in two batches, add more butter for the second batch.)

Sauce

½ cup white cooking wine

8 ounces fresh mushrooms, sliced

2 garlic cloves, crushed or minced

1 (28-ounce) can diced tomatoes

2 tablespoons tomato paste

1 teaspoon brown sugar

½ teaspoon dried basil

½ teaspoon dried parsley flakes

¼ teaspoon salt

¼ teaspoon pepper

⅛ teaspoon red pepper flakes

1 cup shredded mozzarella cheese

¼ cup freshly grated Parmesan cheese

Make sauce: Add wine to pan drippings and reduce to half (about 1 minute). Add mushrooms and garlic and sauté until tender. Add tomatoes, tomato paste, brown sugar, basil, parsley, salt, pepper, and red pepper flakes. Simmer for 10 minutes. Pour sauce over chicken and top with mozzarella cheese and Parmesan cheese. Bake at 350°F for 20 minutes.

Cook spaghetti with 1 teaspoon salt according to package directions. Drain and coat with olive oil. This helps keep it from sticking together.

Serve chicken over pasta and sprinkle with additional freshly grated Parmesan cheese and fresh parsley, if desired.

TIP: To avoid some of the mess of sticky fingers when breading chicken and other meats, try to keep one hand dry and use the other for handling wet ingredients.

TIP: If I have time, I soak the chicken in the buttermilk in the refrigerator for 1–2 hours before coating with breading. Thanks to the enzymes naturally present in buttermilk, soaking in buttermilk tenderizes the chicken.

Chicken Marsala

SERVES 4 – 6

Another Italian classic showcasing mushrooms with a lighter pan sauce.

¾ pound (3 cups) uncooked penne pasta

1 teaspoon salt

1 tablespoon olive oil

3 large chicken breasts

salt and pepper

3 tablespoons butter

½ cup unbleached white flour

1 pound fresh mushrooms, sliced thick

2 large garlic cloves, minced

1 cup marsala wine

1 tablespoon cornstarch

1 cup chicken stock

2 tablespoons cold butter, cubed

1 teaspoon lemon juice

freshly grated Parmesan cheese, to serve

Cook pasta with 1 teaspoon salt according to package directions. Drain and coat with olive oil. This helps keep it from sticking together.

With a sharp knife, slice chicken breasts in half lengthwise. Sprinkle both sides with salt and pepper.

Melt butter in large skillet. Dredge chicken in flour and add to skillet. Fry on medium heat, uncovered, until mostly done, then flip and fry until cooked through (fry 3–4 minutes per side, or until centers reach 165°F). Remove from skillet and place in an oven-safe dish.

Add mushrooms and garlic to pan drippings and sprinkle with salt; add a little butter to pan if needed. Sauté until tender. Add wine and bring to a boil for a few seconds to reduce the alcohol. Dissolve cornstarch in chicken stock and add to pan. Simmer at a rolling boil for 5 minutes, or until the sauce thickens and reduces a bit.

When the sauce is close to done, broil the chicken at 400°F for 3–5 minutes until sizzling hot. This crisps it up a bit but doesn't dry out the meat.

Once sauce is slightly thickened, remove from heat. Add cold butter cubes and whisk until melted. Stir in lemon juice. Season to taste with salt and pepper.

Place hot chicken on a bed of pasta. Pour mushroom sauce over chicken and sprinkle with a little freshly grated Parmesan cheese.

Spring Roll Rice Bowls

with Sweet Garlic and Lime Dressing

SERVES 4

I recently started making rice bowls for my family. This one is full of vibrant flavors. Use the vegetables as a guide and be creative! All the textures and colors make these fun to eat.

2 cups uncooked basmati rice

8 chicken thighs

oil, for pan-frying

Marinade

⅓ cup olive oil

1 tablespoon Dijon mustard

juice of 1 lemon

juice of 1 lime

2 large garlic cloves, crushed or minced

1 tablespoon granulated sugar

1 teaspoon dried parsley flakes

1 teaspoon salt

½ teaspoon pepper

Cook rice according to package directions.

In a 2-cup liquid measuring cup, mix together marinade ingredients. Place chicken thighs in a gallon-sized resealable plastic bag and pour in marinade. Seal bag and flip until chicken is thoroughly coated in marinade. Marinate in refrigerator for 2–4 hours.

In a hot skillet coated with oil, fry the chicken thighs until cooked through. (Alternative: Cook on the grill for about 10 minutes per side, or until centers reach 165°F.) Slice into thin strips while hot and return to your skillet or cover to keep warm.

Vegetables

4 cups sliced red and green cabbage

1 cucumber, sliced

1 red bell pepper, sliced

1 cup chopped tomatoes

½ cup chopped spring onions

1 cup shredded carrots

fresh cilantro

Prepare vegetables and set aside.

Sweet garlic and lime dressing

⅓ cup canola oil

⅓ cup lime juice

¼ cup soy sauce

2 tablespoons rice vinegar

¼ cup brown sugar

2 garlic cloves, crushed

In a bowl, combine dressing ingredients and blend well with an immersible blender.

To assemble: Start with a bed of rice, then top with chicken and vegetables. Drizzle with dressing and sprinkle cilantro over top.

TIP: To get maximum juice from lemons and limes, microwave for 20–30 seconds before squeezing.

Fiesta Burrito Bowls

SERVES 4

A one-dish meal that's great for a last-minute supper.

1½ cup uncooked rice

1 teaspoon salt

6 chicken thighs

2 tablespoons olive oil

1 tablespoon Taco Seasoning (p. 83)

2 cups frozen corn, thawed

1 (15-ounce) can black beans, drained

salt and pepper

Cook rice with 1 teaspoon salt according to package directions.

Cut chicken into 2-inch pieces. In a skillet, fry chicken pieces in oil and sprinkle with taco seasoning. When chicken is cooked through, add corn and black beans. Sprinkle with salt and pepper as desired and simmer until beans are tender. Serve over rice and top with toppings of your choice. I usually use lettuce, tomato, and chopped onion, and drizzle with Ranch Dressing (p. 77).

Honey Barbecue Boneless Wings

SERVES 4 – 6

I love a good boneless chicken wing. This one has a good mix of sweet and spicy heat.

8 boneless, skinless chicken thighs

seasoned salt

flour, for coating chicken

oil, for frying

Barbecue sauce

¼ cup hot sauce

¼ cup ketchup

¼ cup honey

1 tablespoon dark molasses

1 teaspoon lemon juice

¼ teaspoon black pepper

2 dashes garlic powder

2 dashes cayenne pepper

Mix together sauce ingredients and set aside.

Cut chicken thighs into 1½-inch pieces. Sprinkle with seasoned salt and then coat with flour.

In a deep skillet, add 2 inches of oil and heat on medium-high. When oil is hot, add chicken to skillet in batches and fry for 4–5 minutes, turning periodically, until golden brown. Place in a 9-inch baking dish and pour sauce over chicken. Stir to make sure chicken is coated evenly. Broil at 400°F for 10 minutes, stirring halfway.

TIP: To tell whether oil is hot enough, drop in a small piece of bread to see if it bubbles and rises to the top. If so, the oil is ready.

Chicken Potpie

SERVES 4 – 6

If you or anyone in your household wants to be comforted, make this recipe. Chicken potpie is a traditional old-fashioned dish with a flaky crust and creamy filling. If you want a quicker version of this, try Chicken and Dumpling Soup (p. 54).

1 double-crust pastry for a 10-inch pie (p. 226)

Chicken and vegetables

8 boneless, skinless chicken thighs

2 tablespoons butter

1 teaspoon seasoned salt

½ teaspoon pepper

1 cup chopped carrots

½ cup chopped celery

1 cup frozen peas, thawed

Using a 10-inch pie pan, roll out half the pie pastry for the bottom pie crust and use the remaining dough for the top crust.

Cut chicken thighs into 1-inch pieces. In a large saucepan, melt 2 tablespoons butter, add chicken, and sprinkle with seasoned salt and pepper. Cook until no longer pink and starting to brown. Add carrots and celery. Cook until carrots are almost tender. Add peas and cook 1 minute more. Remove chicken and vegetables from saucepan.

Sauce

3 tablespoons butter

1 medium onion, thinly sliced

⅓ cup unbleached white flour

½ teaspoon salt

½ teaspoon pepper

1¾ cup chicken stock

⅔ cup half-and-half

Make sauce: In the same saucepan, melt 3 tablespoons additional butter and add onion. Cook until onion is translucent. Add flour, salt, and pepper and stir until smooth. Stirring continuously, pour in chicken stock and half-and-half. Simmer until thickened. Return chicken and vegetables to the pan and stir until combined.

Egg wash

1 egg, beaten

1 tablespoon water

Fill pie shell with filling. (You may have a little extra; just grab a spoon and help yourself.) Cover the filling with the other rolled-out crust and seal the edges. Cut away excess dough and crimp edges. Make several small slits in the top so steam can escape. In a small bowl, whisk together egg and water and then brush over top of crust.

Bake at 350°F for 45 minutes. Cool 10 minutes before serving so the filling can thicken a little.

Chicken Fajitas

SERVES 6

These chicken fajitas are packed with vibrant flavors and colors. Don't be scared to add the sliced jalapeño—it's not that hot once it's cooked. You could also skip the tortillas and make fajita bowls. This chicken is also delicious when grilled. Simply marinate the chicken thighs whole and slice into strips after grilling.

8 boneless, skinless chicken thighs

1 tablespoon butter

1 onion, sliced

1 green bell pepper, sliced

salt and pepper

6–10 (10-inch) flour tortillas

Marinade

1 jalapeño pepper, sliced

2 garlic cloves, minced or crushed

juice of 1 lime

¼ cup olive oil

1 teaspoon chili powder

1 teaspoon ground cumin

1 teaspoon black pepper

1 teaspoon salt

Slice chicken into ½-inch strips. In a medium bowl, mix together marinade ingredients. Add chicken and toss with marinade. Let stand for 30 minutes.

Melt butter in skillet. Add onion and bell pepper. Sprinkle with salt and pepper. Sauté until tender. Remove from skillet.

Add chicken with marinade to skillet, cover, and cook on medium heat until just done. Return onion and bell pepper to the skillet and simmer, uncovered, for a few minutes. (If it's still really juicy, cook on high until juices reduce.) Heat tortillas. Use tongs to place mixture in tortillas and add toppings of your choice. The possibilities are endless! Try Rice and Beans (p. 135), Ranch Dressing (p. 77), chopped tomatoes, and guacamole.

Mango Chicken Curry

SERVES 6

I created this recipe in order to use up some ripe mangos, and it has been a favorite ever since. It's delightful served with Rice and Beans (p. 135) and thinly sliced cabbage tossed in Classic Creamy Dressing (p. 77).

8 chicken thighs

3 tablespoons olive oil

1 onion, thinly sliced

2 cups chopped fresh mango (may also use frozen)

1 tablespoon lemon juice

fresh basil, for garnish

Seasoning mixture

1 teaspoon salt

1 teaspoon turmeric

1 teaspoon white pepper

1 teaspoon cayenne pepper

Cut chicken into 2-inch pieces. Heat a large skillet and coat well with olive oil. In a small bowl, mix together seasoning mixture. Sprinkle evenly on chicken and stir with hands to make sure chicken is evenly coated. Add chicken to skillet and fry until golden brown.

Add the sliced onions; cover and simmer until onions are tender. Add mango; cover and simmer until mango is soft and juices start to release. Add lemon juice. (If the mixture seems too juicy, uncover and simmer until juices reduce a bit.)

Garnish with fresh basil.

Cajun Chicken

with Avocado

SERVES 4 – 6

Avocados have a way of brightening up any dish.

3 large chicken breasts

1 tablespoon Cajun seasoning

1 teaspoon salt

1 teaspoon pepper

canola oil, for frying

In a small bowl, mix together topping ingredients and refrigerate so flavors can mingle.

With a sharp knife, slice chicken breasts in half lengthwise.

Mix together Cajun seasoning, salt, and pepper. Sprinkle both sides of chicken with seasoning mixture and let stand a few minutes. Heat ⅛ inch of oil in a skillet and fry chicken on medium heat until nearly done, then flip and fry until done (3–4 minutes per side, or until centers reach 165°F).

Avocado topping

3 large avocados, cubed

¼ onion, diced

juice of ½ lemon

salt and pepper, to taste

Serve over Rice and Beans (p. 135) and top with avocado topping.

Grilled Spicy Peach-Glazed Chicken

SERVES 4–6

This dish is a mix of spice and sweet. Go ahead and eat three or more—chicken tenders are small.

2 pounds uncooked chicken tenders

Marinade

½ cup peach preserves

¼ cup oil

2 tablespoons barbecue sauce

1 tablespoon Dijon mustard

1 tablespoon white vinegar

1 large garlic clove, crushed

1 jalapeño pepper, diced

1 teaspoon salt

¼ teaspoon pepper

In a 2-cup liquid measuring cup, mix together marinade ingredients and reserve ¼ cup for glaze. In a gallon-sized resealable plastic bag, add chicken tenders and pour in remaining marinade. Seal bag and flip until chicken is fully coated in marinade. Marinate in refrigerator for 3–4 hours. Grill until cooked through (around 4 minutes per side, or until centers reach 165°F).

Heat reserved marinade in small saucepan to use as a glaze, and drizzle over chicken before serving.

Grilled Honey Mustard Chicken

SERVES 4–6

Everyone loves honey mustard. This chicken is also great sliced on top of a summer garden salad.

8 boneless, skinless chicken thighs

Marinade

⅓ cup honey

3 tablespoons yellow mustard

2 tablespoons white vinegar

1 tablespoon Worcestershire sauce

1 teaspoon poultry seasoning

1 teaspoon salt

½ teaspoon pepper

⅛ teaspoon cayenne pepper

In a 2-cup liquid measuring cup, mix together marinade ingredients and reserve ¼ cup for drizzling at the end. In a gallon-sized resealable plastic bag, add chicken thighs and pour in remaining marinade. Seal bag and flip until chicken is fully coated in marinade. Marinate in refrigerator for 3–4 hours. Grill until cooked through (around 10 minutes per side, or until centers reach 165°F).

Heat reserved marinade and drizzle over chicken before serving.

Grilled Maple Barbecued Chicken

SERVES 4 – 6

A great barbecued chicken dish that is a tasty mix of sweet and smoky.

10 boneless, skinless chicken thighs

Marinade

⅓ cup maple syrup

⅓ cup barbecue sauce

3 tablespoons white vinegar

2 teaspoons Worcestershire sauce

1 teaspoon salt

½ teaspoon dry mustard

¼ teaspoon pepper

In a 2-cup liquid measuring cup, mix together marinade ingredients and reserve ¼ cup for drizzling at the end. In a gallon-sized resealable plastic bag, add chicken thighs and pour in remaining marinade. Seal bag and flip until chicken is fully coated in marinade. Marinate in refrigerator for 3–4 hours. Grill until cooked through (around 10 minutes per side, or until centers reach 165°F).

Heat reserved marinade and drizzle over chicken before serving.

Classic Grilled Chicken

SERVES 4 – 6

This is Joshua's favorite grilled chicken. It also works great with bone-in chicken thighs; just be sure to allow more time for grilling.

8–10 boneless, skinless chicken thighs

Marinade

½ cup water

½ cup white vinegar

⅓ cup canola oil

¼ cup lemon juice

2 large garlic cloves, crushed

1 tablespoon salt

1 teaspoon poultry seasoning

1 teaspoon dried parsley flakes

½ teaspoon pepper

¼ cup honey (optional)

In a 2-cup liquid measuring cup, mix together marinade ingredients. Place chicken thighs in a bowl, add marinade, and toss. Cover and marinate in refrigerator for 6–12 hours. Grill until cooked through (around 10 minutes per side, or until centers reach 165°F).

Grilled Chicken Pitas

SERVES 6

Grilled chicken pitas are great for an outdoor summer party. If you don't like blue cheese, you can omit the blue cheese crumbles. Joshua usually doesn't like blue cheese, but he actually enjoys it in these pitas. You could also use this same recipe with a different dressing. And if you aren't serving these right away, skip tossing the meat and vegetables with the dressing, and serve the dressing on the side.

marinade for Spring Roll Rice Bowls
  (p. 165)

8 boneless, skinless chicken thighs

3 cups chopped fresh vegetables,
  such as:

lettuce

cucumbers

green bell peppers

tomatoes

onions

1 cup Blue Cheese Dressing (p. 79)

½ cup shredded mozzarella cheese

6–7 rounds whole wheat pita bread

Combine marinade ingredients and marinate chicken thighs for 1 hour. Grill until done, then chop chicken into pieces.

In a bowl, mix together grilled chicken, vegetables, and mozzarella cheese.

In another bowl, mix together dressing ingredients. Pour 1 cup dressing over chicken mixture, or just enough so that everything is lightly coated. Toss well. Refrigerate remaining dressing. It should keep for 10 days.

Slice pitas in half and stuff with filling. Makes 12–14 pita halves, depending how full you stuff them.

Cornmeal-Crusted Chicken Tenders

SERVES 4

I like the flavor the cornmeal adds to this recipe. And anything pan-fried in butter tastes good!

1 cup unbleached white flour

⅓ cup cornmeal

1 teaspoon salt

½ teaspoon pepper

1 egg

½ cup buttermilk

¼ cup butter

10 chicken tenders

In a pie pan, combine flour, cornmeal, salt, and pepper. In another pie pan, whisk together egg and buttermilk. Coat chicken tenders with egg mixture, then dredge in flour mixture.

Melt butter in skillet and add chicken tenders. Fry until golden brown, about 4 minutes per side. Serve with dipping sauce of your choice.

NOTE: These can be baked on a baking sheet lined with parchment paper. Spray or brush tops with canola oil and bake at 375°F for 15 minutes.

Crispy Chicken Nuggets

SERVES 4

This a super kid-friendly recipe, but we adults like it too! Serve with Honey Mustard Dressing (p. 80) and you'll have a winner.

canola oil

8 boneless, skinless chicken thighs

1 cup buttermilk

Breading

1 cup unbleached white flour

1 cup panko bread crumbs

1 tablespoon seasoned salt

1 teaspoon paprika

1 teaspoon poultry seasoning

½ teaspoon pepper

Line a baking sheet with parchment paper and coat well with canola oil. Mix together breading ingredients.

Cut chicken into 2-inch pieces. Dip chicken pieces in buttermilk (see tip below), then coat with breading. Place chicken on the baking sheet and spray or brush tops with canola oil. This helps make them crispy.

Bake at 375°F for 20–30 minutes, flipping halfway, or until juices run clear.

TIP: If I have time, I soak the chicken in the buttermilk in the refrigerator for 1–2 hours before coating with breading. Thanks to the enzymes naturally present in buttermilk, soaking in buttermilk tenderizes the chicken.

Honey Roasted Chicken

SERVES 4

Here is a fuss-free way to make chicken for supper.

8 bone-in chicken thighs, skin removed

salt

Lightly salt both sides of chicken thighs.

Sauce

⅓ cup honey

¼ cup canola oil

2 teaspoons lemon juice

1 large garlic clove, crushed

1 teaspoon salt

½ teaspoon pepper

½ teaspoon dried or fresh rosemary

In a 2-cup liquid measuring cup, mix together sauce ingredients.

Place chicken, bone side up, in a 9 x 13-inch pan and pour sauce over it. Let stand for 1 hour. Bake at 375°F for 45 minutes, flipping chicken after 20 minutes.

Herb Roasted Chicken Thighs and Potatoes

SERVES 4

An easy one-dish meal that is full of flavor and color. The chicken melts in your mouth.

8 boneless, skinless chicken thighs

1 onion, cut into chunks

1 sweet potato, cut into chunks

3 red potatoes, cut into chunks

Place chicken and vegetables in a greased large skillet or 9 x 13-inch baking dish.

Sauce

¼ cup butter

4 garlic cloves, crushed

1 teaspoon brown sugar

½ teaspoon salt

½ teaspoon pepper

½ teaspoon poultry seasoning

⅛–¼ teaspoon cayenne pepper

1 tablespoon chopped fresh parsley

In a small saucepan, melt butter and add garlic, brown sugar, salt, pepper, poultry seasoning, cayenne pepper, and parsley. Pour sauce over chicken and vegetables. Toss well with hands to make sure sauce is coated evenly. Bake at 350°F for 1½ hour.

Whole Roasted Chicken

SERVES 4 – 6

Roasting a whole chicken is so easy and can feed a family for two days. Save the leftover meat to make soup or chicken salad and the bones to make your own bone broth.

1 (5- to 6-pound) roasting chicken

salt and pepper

1 head garlic, cut in half crosswise

1 lemon, halved

¼ cup butter, melted

paprika

1 large onion, cut into chunks

4 carrots, cut into 2-inch pieces

olive oil

Remove giblets from chicken cavity and rinse chicken (discard giblets or use in another recipe). Pat chicken dry with a paper towel. Place in a roasting pan. Sprinkle salt and pepper inside cavity and insert the head of garlic and half the lemon. Brush entire chicken liberally with melted butter and squeeze remaining lemon over chicken. Sprinkle all over with paprika, and additional salt and freshly ground pepper.

Place the onions and carrots in the roasting pan around the chicken. Drizzle with oil and sprinkle with salt and pepper. Roast, uncovered, at 425°F for 1½ hour, or until the juices run clear. The internal temperature should reach 165°F. You can cover the pan halfway through to keep it from getting too brown. The skin will still get brown because of the paprika, but don't worry—it's not burnt, it's just full of flavor!

Remove from oven and let rest 10 minutes before serving.

Teriyaki Chicken and Fried Rice

SERVES 4 – 6

My first date with Joshua was at a Japanese steakhouse. We both love Japanese food. Use the vegetable types and amounts in this recipe only as a guide; personally, I like to use whatever vegetables are in season. I also use this recipe with leftover meats. Just add the cooked meat after your vegetables are tender.

2 cups uncooked basmati rice

3 tablespoons oil, divided

8 chicken thighs, cut into strips

salt and pepper

1 medium onion, sliced

3 large carrots, sliced

1 medium zucchini, cut into matchsticks

10 fresh mushrooms, halved

2 eggs

Teriyaki sauce

2 garlic cloves, crushed

¼ teaspoon ginger paste, or 1 teaspoon freshly grated ginger

¼ cup soy sauce

¼ cup water

1 tablespoon rice vinegar

2 tablespoons granulated sugar

1 tablespoon brown sugar

2 teaspoons cornstarch

Cook rice according to package directions and set aside.

In a small saucepan, whisk together teriyaki sauce ingredients and cook until thickened. Set aside.

In a large skillet on medium heat, heat 2 tablespoons oil. When hot, add chicken strips. Sprinkle with salt and pepper. Fry until golden brown. Remove from skillet.

Add 1 tablespoon additional oil to the skillet and add the onions and carrots. (If vegetables start to stick, add a little water to loosen up the bottom.) Sauté until vegetables begin to get tender; then add zucchini and mushrooms. Sauté until all vegetables are tender. Stir in cooked rice.

Make a well in the middle of the rice mixture and crack open the eggs. Stir quickly and scramble into rice mixture. Add cooked chicken and teriyaki sauce. Stir-fry for another 2–3 minutes. Season to taste with salt and pepper.

Yum yum sauce

1 cup mayonnaise

¼ cup ketchup

1 tsp. sriracha sauce

2 tablespoons granulated sugar

¼ teaspoon salt

⅛ teaspoon paprika

In a small bowl, mix together yum yum sauce ingredients and serve on the side.

TIP: This recipe is a great way to use up leftover rice.

Shrimp Alfredo

SERVES 4

A great meal for a special occasion, this dish goes well with Perfect Broccoli (p. 108) and a lettuce salad.

½ pound uncooked fettuccine

1 teaspoon salt

1 tablespoon olive oil

1 tablespoon butter

1 large garlic clove, crushed

1 pound raw shrimp, peeled

salt and pepper

Cook fettuccine with 1 teaspoon salt according to package directions. Drain and coat with olive oil. This helps keep the pasta from sticking together.

In a skillet, melt butter, add garlic, and sauté until fragrant. Add shrimp; sprinkle with salt and pepper. Cook until pink. Remove from skillet.

Sauce

¼ cup white wine

1½ cup milk

½ cup half-and-half

1 tablespoon cornstarch

¼ teaspoon dried basil, or 1 tablespoon chopped fresh basil

¼ cup freshly grated Parmesan cheese

1 teaspoon lemon juice

Add wine to the pan drippings and reduce to half. In a 2-cup or larger liquid measuring pitcher, whisk together milk, half-and-half, and cornstarch. Pour into skillet and simmer until thickened. Add basil and Parmesan cheese and stir until melted.

Return shrimp to skillet and simmer until shrimp are hot. Remove from heat and add lemon juice. Taste for salt and sprinkle in a little more as needed. Serve atop fettuccine.

Classic Steamed Shrimp

SERVES 2 – 4

A classic way to fix shrimp. We have steamed shrimp every Christmas.

1 pound unpeeled shrimp

2 cups water

2 cups white vinegar

¼ cup Old Bay seasoning

2 teaspoons salt

Rinse shrimp. In a pot, heat water, vinegar, Old Bay seasoning, and salt until boiling. Add shrimp. Cover and cook 3 minutes, or until shrimp are pink. Serve immediately with Cocktail Sauce (p. 82).

Citrus Shrimp Kabobs

SERVES 4 – 6

Citrus and Cajun flavors are wonderful on shrimp. I love grilling meats in the summer because it means less mess in the kitchen.

2 pounds raw shrimp, peeled

Sauce

½ cup orange marmalade

½ cup honey

1 tablespoon olive oil

2 tablespoons Cajun seasoning

In a small saucepan, combine sauce ingredients and bring to a boil. Remove from heat. Reserve ½ cup sauce to drizzle over shrimp before serving.

Thread shrimp on kabob sticks and baste with remaining sauce. Let stand 1 hour before grilling.

Grill shrimp until pink and curled. Heat reserved sauce and drizzle over kabobs.

Baked Fish

SERVES 4

Baking fish instead of frying it saves you from cleaning up splattered oil. You can bread the fish when it's partially frozen and let it thaw until you are ready to bake it. I like to use flounder or tilapia in this recipe.

1 cup unbleached white flour

6 fish fillets

Egg wash

3 eggs, beaten

3 tablespoons water

Breading

2 cups panko bread crumbs

1 teaspoon dried dill

2 teaspoons salt

¼ teaspoon pepper

Set out three pie pans. Place flour in one. Whisk together egg wash in another. Mix together breading ingredients in the third pan. (It will be worth the mess, I promise!)

Coat fish with flour, then dip into egg wash, and then into breading. Place on a baking sheet lined with parchment paper and bake at 400°F for 20–22 minutes, until fish flakes easily with a fork or internal temperature reaches 145°F. Serve with Tartar Sauce (p. 80).

Low Country Boil

SERVES 15

A perfect summer meal when sweet corn is just coming in. Low Country Boil is a great meal for larger groups. It can be done inside on the stove in a large pot or outside over a fire in a kettle.

1½ gallon water

¼ cup Old Bay seasoning

1 tablespoon salt

4 pounds small red potatoes

2 pounds kielbasa sausage, cut into 3-inch pieces

12 ears fresh corn, halved

4 large onions, cut into chunks

5 pounds raw shrimp

In a very large pot, add water, Old Bay seasoning, and salt. Bring to a hard boil; add potatoes and cook 10 minutes.

Add kielbasa to pot and cook 10 minutes more. Add corn and cook 3 minutes more. Add onions and cook 2 minutes more. Finally, add shrimp and cook just until pink (around 3 minutes).

Using oven mitts and a large slotted spoon, remove the items from the hot water and place in pans. Spread down the middle of a table covered in newspaper.

Serve with Cocktail Sauce (p. 82), sour cream, butter, and salt and pepper.

Crab Cakes

SERVES 2 – 4

There is nothing like a fresh fried crab cake! Top these with Tartar Sauce (p. 80). Be sure to buy lump crab meat and drain it well! If you don't drain off the liquid, the cakes will fall apart.

2 (6-ounce) cans lump crab meat
¾ cup crushed crackers
1 slice bread, torn into small pieces
¼ cup chopped onion
¼ cup chopped green bell pepper
1 small garlic clove, minced
¼ cup mayonnaise
1 egg, beaten
1 teaspoon lemon juice
½ teaspoon Worcestershire sauce
½ teaspoon Dijon mustard
½ teaspoon Old Bay seasoning
½ teaspoon salt
dash cayenne pepper
flour, for dusting
oil, for frying

Preheat oven to 200°F.

With a strainer, drain crab meat thoroughly. Place crab meat in a medium bowl and add ingredients in order listed, up through cayenne pepper. Mix well. Form patties using ⅓ cup mixture per patty. Dust with flour.

In a deep skillet, add 2 inches of oil and heat on medium-high. When oil is hot, carefully drop crab cakes in oil and fry until brown on both sides (about 4 minutes per side). Rest on a plate lined with paper towels. Then place finished crab cakes on a baking dish in the oven to keep hot until serving.

Serve topped with Tartar Sauce (p. 80).

Sweets

ele

I love sweets, but I don't always make fancy or exotic desserts. I tend to fall back on my old faithful recipes. I like to use whatever fruits are in season. As soon as spring hits, I'm looking forward to rhubarb and strawberry desserts. Come summertime, sour cherries are on my mind. When the cool air moves in, I start dreaming about apple dumplings and ice cream. Winter makes me want to sip hot drinks and nibble on scones and cookies.

Rhubarb Bars

SERVES 12

This is the first rhubarb recipe I make when my rhubarb is ready in early spring. This buttery cake, topped with a rhubarb filling, is what rhubarb lovers' dreams are made of.

1 cup butter, softened

1½ cup granulated sugar

3 eggs

3 cups unbleached white flour

1 teaspoon baking powder

½ teaspoon salt

1 teaspoon vanilla extract

In a stand mixer fitted with the paddle attachment, cream together butter and granulated sugar. Add eggs one at a time and mix well. Add flour, baking powder, salt, and vanilla. Line a 9 x 13-inch baking dish with parchment paper and spread three-quarters of the batter into the baking dish. The batter will be thick.

Filling

1 cup water

1 cup granulated sugar

3 tablespoons cornstarch

3 tablespoons strawberry jam

1 teaspoon vanilla extract

4 cups chopped rhubarb

Make filling: In a saucepan, whisk together water, granulated sugar, and cornstarch. Heat until thickened, remove from heat, and add strawberry jam and vanilla. Add chopped rhubarb and stir. Pour rhubarb mixture over batter in dish and top with remaining batter by adding spoonfuls evenly over the top. Smooth out batter, letting the filling show at some places. Bake at 325°F for 1 hour, or until a wooden pick inserted in the center comes out clean.

Glaze

⅓ cup powdered sugar

2 teaspoons cream

Remove from oven and cool completely. Mix together glaze ingredients and drizzle over bars before serving.

Grandma's Rhubarb Crunch

SERVES 8

A recipe from my grandma Shank that is timeless. Make sure to serve it warm with vanilla ice cream.

4 cups chopped rhubarb

Thickening

1 cup granulated sugar

1 cup water

2 tablespoons cornstarch

2 tablespoons strawberry jam

1 teaspoon vanilla extract

Make thickening: In a saucepan, whisk together granulated sugar, water, and cornstarch and cook until thickened. Remove from heat and add strawberry jam and vanilla. Mix in chopped rhubarb.

Crumbs

1 cup unbleached white flour

1 cup rolled oats

1 cup brown sugar

½ cup melted butter

1 teaspoon ground cinnamon

Make crumbs: In a medium bowl, mix together crumb ingredients. Lightly press half the crumbs into a 9 x 9-inch baking dish. Top with rhubarb mixture. Cover with remaining crumbs. Bake at 350°F for 45 minutes. Serve warm with vanilla ice cream.

Strawberry Shortcake

SERVES 8

I grew up eating this shortcake recipe. It's my grandma's recipe, revised just a little. Every spring, the first bite sure takes me back to my childhood. I love how food can hold memories.

½ cup butter, softened

½ cup sugar

1 egg

1 cup milk

2 cups unbleached white flour

3 teaspoons baking powder

½ teaspoon salt

1 teaspoon vanilla extract

sliced or quartered strawberries

In a medium bowl and using an electric hand mixer, cream together butter and ½ cup sugar. Mix in egg. Add flour, baking powder, salt, and vanilla and beat until just combined. Pour into a greased 9-inch skillet or baking pan. Sprinkle batter with a little additional sugar. Bake at 350°F for 25–30 minutes, or until a wooden pick inserted in the center comes out clean.

Top slices with fresh strawberries and serve with milk.

Cobbler Cake

SERVES 10

Cobbler cake is a great way to use fruit that is in season. Serve with fresh whipped cream or vanilla ice cream.

½ cup butter, softened

1½ cup sugar

4 eggs

2 teaspoons baking powder

1 teaspoon vanilla extract

¼ teaspoon salt

2 cups unbleached white flour

4 cups fresh or frozen fruit

¼–½ cup sugar

In a stand mixer fitted with the paddle attachment, cream together butter and 1½ cup sugar. Add eggs one at a time; then add baking powder, vanilla, salt, and flour in order listed. Mix just until combined.

Grease a 9 x 13-inch baking dish (or line with parchment paper). Spread batter into dish and top with fruit of your choice. Sprinkle top with ¼–½ cup sugar (I gauge the amount by how sweet the fruit is). Bake at 325°F for 1 hour, or until a wooden pick inserted in the middle comes out clean. Baking time will vary depending on the fruit used and whether it's fresh or frozen.

Cream Cheese and Fruit Delight

SERVES 12

Desserts like this one seem to always grace potluck tables. Like lots of other people, I love them too. The crunchy layer, the fluffy cream layer, and then the fruit layer: it's hard to beat. This is a nice dessert for a larger group and a great way to use seasonal fruits. Take your pick of graham cracker, shortbread, or pretzel crust.

Fruit topping of your choice (see instructions)

For fruit topping:

Prepare fresh glazed fruit or pie filling of your choice. You can use the fruit filling for Classic Fruit Pie (p. 229). If so, add 1 cup crushed fresh fruit to the filling mixture before cooking until thickened. Remove from heat and cool to room temperature, then fold in 2 cups fresh fruit. Cool completely before spreading on top of cream cheese filling.

Graham cracker crust

½ cup butter, melted

2½ cups crushed graham crackers (2 packs)

2 tablespoons granulated sugar

For graham cracker crust:

In a small bowl, mix together ingredients with a fork and press firmly into a 9 x 13-inch baking dish. Freeze until firm.

Shortbread crust

1½ cup unbleached white flour

¼ cup granulated sugar

½ cup cold butter, grated

⅛ teaspoon baking powder

⅛ teaspoon baking soda

½ cup chopped pecans

For shortbread crust:

In a small bowl, mix together flour and granulated sugar and cut in butter. Add remaining ingredients. Press into a 9 x 13-inch baking dish and bake at 350°F for 12 minutes. Let cool completely.

Pretzel crust

¾ cup butter, melted

2 cups crushed pretzels

3 tablespoons sugar

For pretzel crust:

In a small bowl, mix together ingredients with a fork. Press firmly into a 9 x 13-inch baking dish and bake at 350°F for 10 minutes. Let cool completely.

Cream cheese filling

1 (8-ounce) package cream cheese, softened

½ cup powdered sugar

1 teaspoon vanilla extract

dash salt

1 pint (2 cups) heavy cream

Make cream cheese filling:

Using a stand mixer fitted with the wire whip, beat cream cheese and powdered sugar until smooth. Add vanilla and salt. Slowly pour in heavy cream and beat on medium-high for 2 minutes, or until stiff peaks form. Spread over cooled crust.

Spread fruit topping over cream cheese filling. Refrigerate before serving.

TIP: This recipe makes 5 cups of cream cheese filling. This filling can be used as a light icing on a cake or as a cream filling for a cake trifle.

Chocolate Cake

with Chocolate Buttercream Frosting

MAKES 1 (9-INCH ROUND) LAYER CAKE

I've made this chocolate cake for years. Joshua asks for this every time his birthday comes around. He never seems to get tired of it. It is very moist, so it's very important to line the cake pan with parchment paper. Sometimes I add fresh fruit on top for a colorful garnish, along with chocolate curls.

2 cups unbleached white flour

2 cups sugar

½ cup cocoa powder

1½ teaspoon baking soda

1 teaspoon baking powder

1 teaspoon salt

1 cup oil

1 cup buttermilk

2 eggs

1 teaspoon vanilla extract

¾ cup hot espresso or strong coffee

Using a stand mixer fitted with the wire whip, mix together ingredients in order listed. (I usually run the mixer on low the whole time I mix up this cake.) Line two (9-inch round) cake pans with parchment paper and spray with baking spray (or use grease and flour). Pour batter equally between the two pans. Bake at 350°F for 30–35 minutes. Do not open the oven door before 30 minutes or the cake may fall. The cake is done when little cracks start appearing on the surface.

Cool 10 minutes, then flip onto parchment paper, and lay on cooling rack.

Chocolate buttercream frosting

½ cup butter

2 cups powdered sugar

½ cup cocoa powder

½ teaspoon vanilla extract

dash salt

¼ cup milk

Remove butter from the refrigerator 30 minutes before starting. (You want it to be room temperature but not too soft.)

Using a stand mixer fitted with the wire whip, beat butter until smooth. Add powdered sugar, cocoa powder, vanilla, salt, and milk. Beat until fluffy (about 2 minutes). After cake is cooled, frost between layers and on top. Refrigerate cake immediately after spreading on frosting.

TIP: I usually make this cake ahead of time and freeze it; I wait to frost the cake until after it is partially thawed. If you prefer a white icing, use the cream cheese filling for Cream Cheese and Fruit Delight (p. 212). If I use that frosting, I add sliced fresh fruit between the layers and garnish the top.

Autumn Apple Cake

with Caramel Icing

MAKES 1 (9 X 13-INCH) CAKE

Every fall I can't wait to make this cake. It's quick to make and can be mixed by hand.

4 cups peeled and chopped apples

1 cup sugar

2 eggs, beaten

½ cup butter, melted

2 cups unbleached white flour

2 teaspoons baking soda

¾ teaspoon salt

1 teaspoon ground cinnamon

¼ teaspoon ground ginger

¼ teaspoon ground nutmeg

1 cup chopped pecans

In a medium bowl, mix together apples and sugar. Let stand for a few minutes, or until apples release their juices. Add eggs and melted butter and mix until combined. In another bowl, mix together flour, baking soda, salt, cinnamon, ginger, nutmeg, and pecans. Add flour mixture to apple mixture and mix until combined. Spread into greased 9 x 13-inch baking dish and bake at 325°F for 35 minutes, or until cake tester or wooden pick inserted in the center comes out clean.

Caramel icing

¼ cup butter

⅓ cup brown sugar

⅛ teaspoon salt

2 tablespoons milk

1 cup powdered sugar

½ teaspoon vanilla extract

In a small saucepan, melt butter and then stir in brown sugar and salt. Cook, stirring, until the sugar melts. Add the milk, bring to a boil, and pour into a mixing bowl to cool for 10 minutes.

After 10 minutes, stir in the powdered sugar and vanilla. Whisk until smooth. Spread over warm cake.

Apple Cinnamon Shortbread Bars

MAKES 12 BARS

I love shortbread crusts. The cinnamon cream cheese paired with the sugared apples makes a delightful harmony of fall flavors. I use Gala apples in this recipe.

Crust

¼ cup chopped pecans

1½ cup unbleached white flour

¼ cup granulated sugar

⅛ teaspoon baking powder

⅛ teaspoon baking soda

½ cup butter, melted

Make crust: In a small bowl, combine crust ingredients. Firmly press into a 9 x 13-inch baking dish and set aside.

Filling

1 (8-ounce) package cream cheese, softened

¼ cup brown sugar

½ teaspoon ground cinnamon

1 teaspoon vanilla extract

Make filling: In a medium bowl and using an electric mixer, beat together filling ingredients until smooth. Carefully spread over crust. (Start with small spoonfuls all over the crust to prevent the crust from pulling up while spreading. An angled spatula works best.)

Apple topping

2–3 apples, peeled and sliced

2 tablespoons granulated sugar

¼ teaspoon ground cinnamon

Layer apple slices evenly on top of the cream cheese filling. In a small bowl, combine granulated sugar and cinnamon. Sprinkle over apples. Bake at 350°F for 35–40 minutes, or until apples are tender. Cool completely before cutting into squares and serving. Refrigerate after serving.

TIP: You can also make this recipe in a 10-inch springform pan. It's a more elegant version for guests. I've used pears for the topping as well.

Apple Dumplings

MAKES 14 DUMPLINGS

Apple dumplings are like little packages of fall. There is something special about them; maybe it's the time and effort you know someone put into making them. Gala apples are perfect for this recipe.

2x double-crust pie pastry (p. 226)
8 apples, peeled, halved, and cored
brown sugar
ground cinnamon
butter

Divide pie dough in half. Roll one half into a 14 x 18-inch rectangle. Lay half the apples on top of the dough, spaced apart and cut side up. Cut squares of dough around them with a knife, just large enough to cover the apple. (Cut one square to see if you are estimating the right size.)

Fill each apple center with a rounded teaspoon of brown sugar and a dash cinnamon. Top with a small dab of butter. Fold ends of dough squares to the center of the apple and pinch edges together. Place in a 9 x 13-inch baking dish with the flat side down so the seams are on the bottom. Repeat with remaining dough and apples, placing in a second baking dish.

Sauce
1 cup granulated sugar
1 cup brown sugar
3 cups water
½ teaspoon ground cinnamon
½ teaspoon ground nutmeg
¼ cup butter

In a saucepan, combine sauce ingredients except for butter. Heat to boiling. Remove from heat and add butter.

Divide sauce in half and pour over each baking dish of dumplings. Bake at 375°F for 35 minutes. Serve warm with ice cream.

Caramel Apples

I've made big batches of these caramel apples to sell for a few fall events in our area. Now, at home, it's fun to make sixteen instead of two hundred!

16 small apples

16 wooden sticks

Wash apples and dry well. Push a wooden stick into the center of each apple. Line a baking sheet with parchment paper and grease with baking spray or butter.

Caramel

2¼ cups brown sugar

½ cup butter

1 cup dark corn syrup

1 (14-ounce) can sweetened condensed milk

¼ teaspoon salt

1 teaspoon vanilla extract

In a heavy saucepan, combine all the caramel ingredients except the vanilla. Cook over medium heat until sugar dissolves. Increase heat and cook, stirring constantly, until mixture reaches 240°F on a candy thermometer. Remove from heat and cool to 200°F. Stir in vanilla. Quickly dip apples in caramel sauce and place on greased parchment paper. Place in freezer until hardened. Place in bags and store in refrigerator for up to 1 week.

Caramel Custard

When I was growing up, we often served this silky custard when company came to our home.

1¼ cup brown sugar

½ cup butter

2 tablespoons cold water

7½ cups milk, divided

3 eggs, beaten

⅔ cup cornstarch

½ cup unbleached white flour

1 teaspoon salt

1 tablespoon unflavored gelatin

¼ cup water

2 teaspoons vanilla extract

In a skillet, caramelize brown sugar and butter until fragrant. Remove from heat. Add 2 tablespoons cold water and stir until smooth.

Pour 7 cups milk into a large saucepan. Whisk in the caramel mixture, stirring constantly, and heat to almost boiling.

In a 2-cup liquid measuring cup, whisk together remaining ½ cup milk, eggs, cornstarch, flour, and salt until smooth. Add to hot milk mixture while stirring, and heat until thickened. Remove from heat.

Dissolve gelatin in ¼ cup additional water. Add dissolved gelatin and vanilla to custard. Blend with an immersible blender and then refrigerate until set. Before serving, whip with an electric hand mixer until smooth.

Pie Crust

Here's my favorite pie crust recipe, which makes either two pies (bottom crust only) or one pie (with a top crust). Making pie crust is often considered to be complicated. But if you've only tried it once or twice, don't give up just yet. Practice makes perfect. You will learn helpful techniques the more often you make pie crust. My tips? Do not add too much water and do not overwork the dough.

2½ cups unbleached white flour

1 teaspoon salt

10 tablespoons cold butter

¼ cup cold lard or shortening

8–10 tablespoons ice water (approximately)

In a stand mixer fitted with the paddle attachment, mix together flour and salt. Grate butter and return to the refrigerator. Measure the lard and get the ice water ready. Remove butter from the refrigerator.

Start mixer on medium speed. Add lard in small spoonfuls, then add grated butter in small handfuls. Mix until the biggest butter clump is the size of a large pea. Remove bowl from mixer stand. (You can also do this step with a hand pastry blender.)

Using a fork to gently mix dough, add ice water 1 tablespoon at a time. Important: As soon as you see the dough come together, stop adding water. You can press the dough together with your hands and see if it stays together. It's okay if there are some dry clumps in the bottom of the bowl. Dump dough on the counter and work it with your hands until it stays together, adding tiny amounts of water if needed.

Form dough into two rounds. Refrigerate for 1–2 hours. Roll out into two large circles and place in pie pans. Cut edges and crimp as you desire.

To bake the crust before filling it, prick the crust all over with a fork to let the heat escape. Carefully line your pie shell with foil to help hold the sides up while baking. Bake at 375°F for 8 minutes. Remove foil and bake 10 minutes more. If crust starts to bubble up, prick with a fork until bubbles deflate, then continue baking.

Classic Fruit Pie

MAKES 1 (9-INCH) PIE

This recipe can be used with almost any fruit, fresh or frozen. I have found that if you use frozen fruit, the fruit still tastes really fresh.

1 (9-inch) unbaked pie shell

Fruit filling

1 cup water

¾ cup sugar

¼ cup Clear Jel

¼ teaspoon salt

1 teaspoon almond flavoring, or
   1 tablespoon lemon juice

3–4 cups cut fruit (4 cups for a deep-
   dish pie)

In a small saucepan, mix together water, sugar, Clear Jel, and salt. Cook until thickened. Remove from heat. Add either almond flavoring or lemon juice, depending on which you think tastes best with the fruit you are using. Fold in fruit and pour into unbaked pie shell.

Crumb topping

⅓ cup unbleached white flour

¼ cup sugar

3 tablespoons cold butter, grated

Prepare crumb topping: In a small bowl mix together flour and sugar. Cut in butter until crumbs form. Sprinkle evenly on top of fruit filling. Bake at 350°F for 45–55 minutes.

TIP: Here is a great way to know your fruit pie is done: the filling needs to bubble for at least 6–10 minutes to properly cook the fruit.

Fresh Strawberry Pie

MAKES 2 (9-INCH) PIES

Every time strawberry season came around during my childhood, we all eagerly anticipated this pie.

2 (9-inch) pie shells, baked

Fruit filling

2 cups water

¾ cup granulated sugar

3 tablespoons Clear Jel

dash salt

1 (3-ounce) box strawberry gelatin

10 cups sliced fresh strawberries

Make filling: In a small saucepan, stir together water, granulated sugar, Clear Jel, and salt. Cook until thickened. Remove from heat and add strawberry gelatin. Let cool to room temperature, then add sliced strawberries. Pour into two baked pie shells and refrigerate until set.

Whipped cream

1 pint (2 cups) heavy cream

½ cup powdered sugar

½ teaspoon vanilla extract

pinch salt

Make whipped cream: In a medium bowl and using an electric mixer, beat together whipped cream ingredients until peaks form. Dollop on pies before serving.

Peanut Butter Pie

MAKES 1 (9-INCH) PIE

My mom is known far and wide for her peanut butter pie. Topped with fluffy whipped cream and clusters of peanut butter crumbs, this silky custard pie boasts the perfect textures.

1 (9-inch) pie shell, baked

Custard
2½ cups milk, divided
⅓ cup granulated sugar
¼ cup cornstarch
¼ cup unbleached white flour
¼ teaspoon salt
3 eggs yolks, beaten
2 teaspoons gelatin
¼ cup cold water
1 tablespoon butter
1 teaspoon vanilla extract

Make custard: In a double boiler, heat 2 cups milk until steamy. In a small bowl, combine remaining ½ cup milk with sugar, cornstarch, flour, and salt. Whisk until smooth or blend with an immersible blender. While stirring milk on stove, pour in cornstarch mixture. Stir constantly and cook until custard is thickened.

Temper eggs yolks by stirring a small amount of hot custard into egg yolks. Stirring constantly, add yolk mixture to hot custard and cook for about 3 minutes. Remove from heat.

Dissolve gelatin in ½ cup cold water. Add butter, vanilla, and dissolved gelatin to hot custard. Stir well. Refrigerate until set; it will be very stiff.

Crumbs
¾ cup powdered sugar
½ cup peanut butter

Make crumbs: In a small bowl, mix powdered sugar and peanut butter until crumbs form. Refrigerate until ready to use.

Several hours before serving, whip custard with a hand mixer until smooth. Sprinkle about two-thirds of the crumbs into the baked pie shell. Reserve the remaining crumbs. Pour whipped custard over crumbs in pie shell. Return to the refrigerator for several hours so custard can set again.

Whipped cream
1 pint (2 cups) heavy cream
½ cup powdered sugar
½ teaspoon vanilla extract
pinch salt

Make whipped cream: In a medium bowl and using an electric mixer, beat together whipped cream ingredients until stiff peaks form. Spread on pie. Garnish with reserved peanut butter crumbs.

Maple Pecan Pie

MAKES 1 (9-INCH) PIE

I love this recipe because it uses maple syrup instead of corn syrup. The whiskey is optional; it adds another layer of flavor.

1 (9-inch) unbaked pie shell

Filling

1 cup maple syrup

1 tablespoon whiskey (optional)

3 large eggs

3 tablespoons butter, melted

1 teaspoon vanilla extract

¾ cup brown sugar

2 tablespoons unbleached white flour

¼ teaspoon salt

1½ cup chopped pecans

In a bowl, whisk together all filling ingredients except the pecans. Place pecans in unbaked pie shell and pour syrup mixture over pecans. Bake at 350°F for 45–50 minutes, or until top starts to puff up and center seems set.

Pumpkin Pie

MAKES 1 (9-INCH) PIE

This is my mom's pumpkin pie recipe, which she originally got from a neighbor. This pie has been present at every Thanksgiving meal for as long as I can remember.

1 (9-inch) unbaked pie shell

Filling

2 eggs

½ cup milk

½ cup cream

1½ cup pumpkin puree

½ cup brown sugar

½ teaspoon salt

1 teaspoon ground cinnamon

½ teaspoon ground ginger

¼ teaspoon ground cloves

1 teaspoon vanilla extract

Blend all filling ingredients in a blender and pour into unbaked pie shell. Bake at 400°F for 15 minutes, reduce heat to 350°F, and bake 30 minutes more, or until center registers 175°F. The center will still be wobbly but will set as it cools. You can also test for doneness by inserting a knife about 1 inch away from the crust's edge; if it comes out clean, it's done.

Pumpkin Bars

with Cream Cheese Frosting

MAKES 20 BARS

This recipe from my grandma Shank is great for fall parties. Mom used to make these for our youth group parties, and she would top each square with a candy pumpkin.

1 cup oil

2 cups granulated sugar

4 eggs, beaten

2 cups pumpkin puree

2 teaspoons salt

2 teaspoons ground cinnamon

1 teaspoon baking soda

1 teaspoon baking powder

2 cups unbleached white flour

1 teaspoon vanilla extract

In a medium bowl and using an electric mixer, mix together batter ingredients in order listed. Pour batter into a greased and floured 13 x 18-inch baking sheet. Bake at 350°F for 20–25 minutes. Cool before spreading on frosting.

Frosting

1 (8-ounce) package cream cheese, softened

¼ cup butter, softened

2½ cups powdered sugar

1 teaspoon vanilla extract

dash salt

Make frosting: In a small bowl, use an electric mixer to beat together cream cheese and butter until smooth. Add powdered sugar, vanilla, and salt. Beat until fluffy and smooth. Spread on cooled bars.

Chocolate Zucchini Bars

SERVES 12

These bars are a great way to use up zucchini, that overabundant garden vegetable. There are no eggs in this recipe. Enjoy with a cold glass of milk.

2 cups shredded zucchini

1½ cup sugar

½ cup oil

2 cups unbleached white flour

½ cup cocoa powder

1½ teaspoon baking soda

1 teaspoon salt

In a large bowl, mix together zucchini, sugar, and oil. Add remaining ingredients and mix well. Spread into a greased 9 x 13-inch baking dish. Bake at 350°F for 30 minutes. Cool and then spread with ganache frosting.

Whipped ganache frosting

½ cup heavy cream

1 cup semisweet chocolate chips

In a small saucepan, heat heavy cream and chocolate chips until smooth. Refrigerate until just chilled but not stiff. With an electric mixer, beat until peaks form. Spread on cooled bars. Refrigerate before serving.

Peanut Butter Bars

MAKES ABOUT 20 BARS

I have a hard time not eating these bars when they are present in my kitchen. The marriage of chocolate and peanut butter makes them irresistible.

1 cup butter, softened

¾ cup granulated sugar

¾ cup brown sugar

2 eggs

½ cup peanut butter

1 teaspoon salt

1 teaspoon baking soda

1 teaspoon vanilla extract

2 cups unbleached white flour

2 cups rolled oats

Using a stand mixer fitted with the paddle attachment, cream together butter, granulated sugar, and brown sugar. Add eggs and peanut butter and beat until fluffy. Add remaining batter ingredients and mix until just combined. Spread out batter evenly on a greased 13 x 18-inch baking sheet. Bake at 350°F for 15–18 minutes, or just until starting to brown at the edges. Do not overbake.

Topping

1 cup semisweet chocolate chips

½ cup peanut butter

Melt chocolate chips in a small saucepan, or place in a bowl and microwave for 30 seconds. Stir in peanut butter. Spread on top of warm bars, then refrigerate until chocolate topping is set. Cut into squares and enjoy!

Granola Bars

These granola bars make a great snack or item for packed lunches. Children can help make them too.

4½ cups crispy rice cereal

2 cups rolled oats

9 graham crackers, crushed

½ cup chopped pecans

½ cup dried cranberries

½ cup shredded sweetened coconut

2 tablespoons wheat germ

¼ teaspoon salt

¼ cup butter

1 (10½-ounce) bag mini marshmallows

¼ cup honey

¼ cup peanut butter

½ cup chocolate chips

In a large bowl, mix together crispy rice cereal, rolled oats, crushed graham crackers, chopped pecans, cranberries, coconut, wheat germ, and salt.

In a saucepan, melt butter and marshmallows. Remove from heat and add honey and peanut butter. Pour melted mixture over cereal mixture, stirring constantly. Once everything sticks together, press mixture evenly into a greased 13 x 18-inch baking sheet. Sprinkle chocolate chips on top of bars. Top with a piece of greased wax paper and roll with a rolling pin to press chocolate chips into the mixture (this step avoids mixing the chocolate chips into the hot marshmallow mixture, which would cause the chocolate to melt). Cut into rectangles.

Sugar Cookies

MAKES 8–9 DOZEN DEPENDING ON COOKIE CUTTER SIZE

When I think of Christmas cookies, I imagine these sugar cookies. Mom would make them every year. I still remember opening the squeaky door of our chest freezer to sneak one to eat with Dad's hot chocolate.

1½ cup butter, softened

2 cups granulated sugar

6 egg yolks

1 cup sour cream

1 teaspoon vanilla extract

2 teaspoons baking powder

1½ teaspoon baking soda

1 teaspoon salt

6 cups all-purpose flour

Make cookies: In a stand mixer fitted with the paddle attachment, cream together butter and granulated sugar. Add egg yolks and sour cream. Mix in vanilla. In another bowl, sift together baking powder, baking soda, salt, and flour. Add egg mixture and mix just until combined. Refrigerate for 2 hours. Roll out dough ¼ inch thick and cut into shapes. Bake at 350°F for 8–10 minutes. Do not allow to brown. Cool completely before icing.

Icing

1 cup butter, softened

1 teaspoon vanilla extract

⅛ teaspoon salt

1 egg yolk (optional; it will not be cooked)

6 cups powdered sugar

Make icing: In a stand mixer fitted with the wire whip, cream together butter, vanilla, salt, and egg yolk, if desired. Add powdered sugar and beat until creamy. Add a little milk if the icing seems too thick. Ice cookies. If you don't plan to serve them right away, freeze to keep fresh.

Chocolate Chip Cookies

MAKES 4–5 DOZEN

This is the only cookie recipe my husband asks me to make. He claims there is no other cookie like this one. I freeze them in small bags for him to take to work for lunch. If you don't have lard on hand, you can substitute it with an additional ½ cup softened butter.

½ cup butter, softened

½ cup lard

1 cup granulated sugar

1 cup brown sugar

3 eggs

2 teaspoons baking powder

2 teaspoons baking soda

2 teaspoons vanilla extract

½ teaspoon salt

3½ cups unbleached white flour

1 cup semisweet chocolate chips

Using a stand mixer fitted with the paddle attachment, cream together butter, lard, granulated sugar, and brown sugar. Add remaining ingredients in order listed and mix just until combined.

Using a 1½-inch cookie scoop, scoop onto a baking sheet lined with parchment paper. Bake at 350°F for 8–9 minutes, or just until the tops are starting to brown. The cookies will look a little wet, but as they cool, they will become chewy and just right.

TIP: It's always good to bake two to three cookies for a test bake before baking the whole batch. That way, if your cookies fall flat, you have time to work in a little more flour before baking the rest.

Chewy Oatmeal Cookies

MAKES ABOUT 5 DOZEN

I don't make lots of different kinds of cookies; I'd rather have a couple of favorites. That way, deciding which kind of cookies to make is simple! These are the "other cookie" I make, besides chocolate chip. They are delightfully crunchy and chewy at the same time. Be sure to use rolled oats; quick oats will make a dry cookie. If you don't have lard on hand, you can substitute it with an additional ½ cup softened butter.

½ cup butter, softened
½ cup lard
1 cup brown sugar
1 cup granulated sugar
2 eggs
1 teaspoon baking soda
1 teaspoon ground cinnamon
1 teaspoon vanilla extract
½ teaspoon salt
¾ cup raisins or dried cranberries
4½ cups rolled oats
1 cup unbleached white flour
½ cup shredded sweetened coconut

Using a stand mixer fitted with the paddle attachment, cream together butter, lard, brown sugar, and granulated sugar. Add remaining ingredients in order listed and mix until just combined. Refrigerate dough for 1 hour.

Using a 1½-inch cookie scoop, scoop onto a baking sheet lined with parchment paper. Bake at 350°F for 10–11 minutes. Underbaked, they fall flat; overbaked, they aren't as chewy. I find that 11 minutes is perfect. Even if they seem a little wet, they will set up once they cool.

Glazed Doughnuts

MAKES 6–7 DOZEN

I make these doughnuts every time we have a snow day. It means I usually plan to be in the kitchen most of the day, but the reward is great. These doughnuts also freeze well to be enjoyed later—which is good, as this is a large recipe!

5 tablespoons active dry yeast

1 tablespoon sugar

1 cup warm water

1½ cup sugar

1 cup butter, softened

5 eggs, beaten

4 teaspoons salt

2 teaspoons vanilla extract

2 teaspoons ground nutmeg

15 cups unbleached white flour

4 cups water

lard or oil, for frying

In a medium bowl, dissolve yeast and 1 tablespoon sugar in 1 cup warm water. Set aside.

In a very large bowl and using an electric hand mixer, cream together 1½ cup sugar and butter. Add eggs, salt, vanilla, and nutmeg. Mix until combined, then add yeast mixture. Add flour alternately with 4 cups water. (I use my small hand mixer for the first few cups of flour, and then I use a wooden spoon to mix in the rest of the flour.) This will be a fairly sticky dough, which makes a tender doughnut. Cover and let rise until doubled. Punch down, then let rise again until doubled.

Sprinkle flour on your workspace. Divide the dough in half and roll out to ½ inch thick. Cut circles with a doughnut cutter and lay on a lightly floured surface. Stretch out doughnut centers as you lay them down. This helps the holes remain open as the doughnuts rise. Repeat with remaining dough. Let rise until doubled in size.

In a large bowl, mix together glaze ingredients until smooth. Set aside.

In a deep electric skillet, heat lard or oil to 375°F.

Add doughnuts to skillet with the top, risen side facing down in the oil. This helps the bottom side rise while you are frying the top side. Flip to fry each side until golden brown. Lay on paper towels for a minute or so.

Glaze

4 pounds powdered sugar

¼ cup cornstarch

2 cups milk

2 teaspoons vanilla extract

⅛ teaspoon salt

Place doughnuts in a row on a wooden stick or wooden spoon handle. Lay across glaze bowl and pour glaze over doughnuts with a ladle. Let drip for a few minutes and then place doughnuts on trays. Eat as many as you can; they are best when they are fresh! Freeze the rest in airtight containers for another snowy day.

TIP: It's important to maintain a temperature of 375°F when you are frying the doughnuts; at this temperature, the oil seals the outside of the doughnut so oil doesn't soak in. If the oil is too hot, the doughnut will get too brown and crispy on the outside before the inside has cooked through. If the oil is not hot enough, the doughnut will absorb too much oil and the texture will be soggy and greasy.

Protein Balls

I've found myself mixing up this recipe many evenings after nine o'clock. It's usually because I'm hankering for a bedtime snack. These balls are also great for an afternoon pick-me-up with iced coffee. If you are rushed for time, you can skip melting the chocolate chips and just add them to the main filling.

1½ cup crispy rice cereal

1½ cup rolled oats

⅔ cup shredded sweetened coconut

½ cup dried cranberries

¼ teaspoon salt

1 cup peanut butter

½ cup honey

2 tablespoons protein powder
  (optional)

Using a stand mixer fitted with the paddle attachment, mix together ingredients except those for the topping until well combined. Using a small cookie scoop, form balls. Place on a baking sheet lined with parchment paper. Place in the freezer until firm, about 10 minutes.

Topping

½ cup semisweet chocolate chips

sea salt

Melt chocolate chips and drizzle over protein balls with a fork. Sprinkle with sea salt.

Three-Colored Coconut Candy

Three-colored coconut candy is Joshua's favorite Christmas candy. It is a wonderful candy with an interesting texture—the gelatin makes it slightly spongy.

First layer

1½ tablespoon unflavored gelatin

3 tablespoons water

2 cups sugar

1 cup milk

1 tablespoon butter

dash salt

1¼ cup shredded sweetened coconut

1 teaspoon vanilla extract

Second layer

1½ tablespoon unflavored gelatin

3 tablespoons water

2 cups sugar

1 cup milk

1 tablespoon butter

dash salt

1¼ cup shredded sweetened coconut

1 teaspoon vanilla extract

⅛ teaspoon red food color

Third layer

1½ tablespoon unflavored gelatin

3 tablespoons water

2 cups sugar

1 cup milk

1 tablespoon butter

dash salt

1¼ cup shredded sweetened coconut

1 teaspoon vanilla extract

3 tablespoons cocoa powder

All three layers use the same base mixture, but the second and third layers include the addition of red food color and cocoa powder, respectively. Thus you will prepare a variation of the base layer three times.

In a small bowl, dissolve 1½ tablespoon gelatin in 3 tablespoons water and set aside.

In a medium saucepan, combine 2 cups sugar, 1 cup milk, 1 tablespoon butter, and a dash salt and heat to boiling. Stirring constantly, boil to 232°F. Remove from heat.

Using a stand mixer fitted with the wire whip, add dissolved gelatin to mixing bowl and pour in hot sugar-and-milk mixture. Mix on medium-high for about 4 minutes. The mixture will turn white and creamy. Add 1¼ cup coconut and 1 teaspoon vanilla. Beat until coconut is mixed in.

Pour into greased 9 x 13-inch dish. (The mixture will be a similar consistency to that of melted marshmallows—you will need to use a spoon to spread it out.)

Repeat the process for the second and third layers. For the second layer, add red food color along with the coconut and vanilla; spread on top of the first layer. For the third layer, add cocoa powder along with the coconut and vanilla; spread on top of the second layer.

When the layers are set, invert the dish onto a cutting board and remove the pan. Cut into small pieces. Store in resealable plastic bags and freeze to retain freshness.

Peanut Butter Balls

Here is a simple candy I make every Christmas. Adding the cream cheese to the filling helps keep these candies nice and creamy.

3½ cups powdered sugar

1½ cup peanut butter

4 ounces cream cheese, softened

½ cup butter, softened

1 teaspoon vanilla extract

¼ teaspoon salt

Make balls: Use your hands to mix together powdered sugar, peanut butter, cream cheese, butter, vanilla, and salt until blended. Refrigerate for 10–15 minutes, or until firm. Use a small cookie scoop to form balls. Place on wax paper and place in freezer until firm.

Chocolate coating

dark chocolate, melted

milk chocolate, melted

sea salt or fleur de sel

Dip into melted dark chocolate, then return to freezer until hardened. Drizzle with milk chocolate. Sprinkle with sea salt. Store in the freezer.

Chocolate Bark

SERVES 6

I make chocolate bark every Christmas. It's easy to make, and it's so good. I usually give a box of homemade candy to family members. I include this chocolate bark along with Peanut Butter Balls (above), and Three-Colored Coconut Candy (p. 257).

10 ounces dark chocolate

10 ounces milk chocolate

½ cup coarsely chopped dried cranberries

½ cup chopped pecans

fleur de sel or sea salt

fresh orange zest

In a double boiler, melt dark chocolate. Pour melted chocolate into the middle of a baking sheet lined with parchment paper. Spread into a rectangle 3–4 inches from the edge of the tray. Place tray in the freezer to chill.

In a double boiler, melt milk chocolate. Remove tray from the freezer and pour three-quarters of the milk chocolate over the dark chocolate, spreading to the edges of the hardened chocolate. Sprinkle on dried cranberries and pecans. With a fork, drizzle the remaining milk chocolate across the rectangle, then sprinkle with fleur de sel. Finally, grate on some fresh orange zest. Place in the freezer until set, then break into pieces.

Box for a Christmas gift or place in the freezer for later.

Kitchen Tips
and Measurements

Taste your food as you cook

Even if I use the same recipe and follow it every time, I still always taste the final dish for salt and sprinkle in a little if needed. I think one of the things that makes a good cook is having the taste buds for the end result.

Use quality spices

Spices are a small thing that make a big difference. Compare a generic brand and a name-brand spice; the color will be different, as will the smell and taste. Bulk food stores usually have quality spices at reasonable prices.

Shred your own cheese

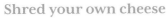

It's cheaper per pound and tastes better. Once you get in the habit of shredding your own, you won't even be tempted to buy pre-shredded.

Use fresh garlic

There is no comparison between the taste of fresh garlic and that of garlic powder. An easy way to peel a bunch of cloves at a time is to put them in a pint jar, cover with a lid, and shake vigorously. The skins will pop right off. A garlic press is a great way to crush garlic quickly and add it to a dish. Daintily mincing each clove with a knife is fine, but it takes time.

Use real buttermilk

I know it's handy to quickly sour some milk with vinegar when a recipe calls for buttermilk. But it will never measure up to real buttermilk. Buttermilk will keep about 2 weeks in the refrigerator.

Test your oven temperature accuracy with a separate oven thermometer

You can purchase one for under ten dollars. This eliminates lots of frustration for many cooks.

Use digital scales

These are especially helpful when feeding your sourdough starter equal amounts. One cup of water weighs more than one cup of flour. And if you shop at stores that sell groceries in bulk, after you're home it's handy to weigh out 8 ounces from a 32-ounce bag of something. I also use digital scales for weighing dough for pie crusts or shaping rolls to be sure they are equally divided.

Weights and measures

These are not exact equivalents, but have been rounded up or down for easier measuring.

⅛ teaspoon	0.5 ml	-	-
¼ teaspoon	1 ml	-	-
½ teaspoon	2 ml	-	-
1 teaspoon	5 ml	-	-
1 tablespoon	3 teaspoons	½ fluid ounce	15 ml
2 tablespoons	⅛ cup	1 fluid ounce	30 ml
4 tablespoons	¼ cup	2 fluid ounces	60 ml
5⅓ tablespoons	⅓ cup	3 fluid ounces	80 ml
8 tablespoons	½ cup	4 fluid ounces	120 ml
10⅔ tablespoons	⅔ cup	5 fluid ounces	160 ml
12 tablespoons	¾ cup	6 fluid ounces	180 ml
16 tablespoons	1 cup	8 fluid ounces	240 ml
2 cups	1 pint	-	-
2 pints	1 quart	-	-
4 quarts	1 gallon	-	-
28 grams	1 ounce	-	-
1 kilogram	2.2 pounds	-	-
1 liter	1 quart	-	-
4 liters	1 gallon	-	-

Use a digital instant-read thermometer

I frequently use a thermometer for testing to see if things are done. For instance, bread is done at 195°F and meat loaf is done at 160°F. Even though Grandma always baked meat loaf for an hour at 350°F, a 1-pound loaf is actually done in around 35 minutes. You will find meat loaf and meatballs are more tender and less dense when not overbaked. A thermometer also eliminates the guessing game for when meats are done. Even though my mom still thinks pork chops can't be a bit pink, I remind her that when the thermometer reaches 145°F, they are safe for her to eat and serve.

Safe minimum internal meat temperatures

Beef, Pork, Veal & Lamb Steaks, chops, roasts	**145°F (62.8°C)** and allow to rest for at least 3 minutes
Ground Meats	**160°F (71.1°C)**
Ham fresh or smoked (uncooked)	**145°F (62.8°C)** and allow to rest for at least 3 minutes
Fully Cooked Ham (to reheat)	Reheat cooked hams packaged in USDA-inspected plants to **140°F (60°C)** and all others to **165°F (73.9°C)**.
All Poultry (breasts, whole bird, legs, thighs, wings, ground, giblets, and stuffing)	**165°F (73.9°C)**
Eggs	**160°F (71.1°C)**
Fish & Shellfish	**145°F (62.8°C)**
Leftovers	**165°F (73.9°C)**
Casseroles	**165°F (73.9°C)**

Oven temperature equivalents

250°F	120°C
275°F	135°C
300°F	150°C
325°F	160°C
350°F	180°C
375°F	190°C
400°F	200°C
425°F	220°C
450°F	230°C
475°F	240°C

Create a baking corner in your kitchen

I love to bake. My sister Faith claimed she didn't. Every time I went to bake something in her kitchen, I went zigzagging across her kitchen to find oats, oil, and flour. I told her that I wouldn't like baking either if I had to run everywhere to find my ingredients! So I went to her home one day and helped make her a baking corner, in which all her baking ingredients would be within arm's reach. I labeled quart jars and poured a common baking ingredient into each one. We moved her mixer, measuring cups, and spoons to her new baking corner. She called the next day to say she was amazed at how enjoyable baking really was!

Acknowledgments

The first thanks goes to my sister Faith, who told me I could do this project with young children. She also came many days to help with housework and to keep my girls while I wrote. She was also a great encourager and helped me not overthink this book: just to do my best and be done.

Also, a big thank-you to my husband, Joshua, who encouraged me through this whole project and told me I could do this cookbook. You and the girls were so patient about waiting on your supper while I photographed it fifty times before you could eat it. You will always be my favorite person to cook for.

To my own mom, Sandra, who taught me so much about food. I give you 90 percent of the credit for this cookbook. And to my dad, Elvin, who taught me that hard work never hurt anyone and to keep going until a project is done.

To my other sister, Charity, who encouraged me with phone calls from Indiana. I promise I don't mind if you still don't use my fajita recipe.

To my good mom friend Kim, who tested recipes and listened to my many cookbook dilemmas. Thanks for being a listening ear and encouraging me along the way.

A big thank-you to all my recipe testers: Suetta, Angie, Kim, Jessica, Charity, and Faith. You don't know how much I valued your feedback while testing recipes. You helped with one of the biggest jobs I had. Thank you from the bottom of my heart.

The final and biggest thank-you goes to my editor, Valerie. Your grace, wisdom, and patience throughout this project gave me the encouragement and insight I needed to press on.

Index

The Author

Hope Helmuth is a Mennonite cook, mother, and blogger who enjoys creating recipes, entertaining guests, gardening, graphic design, and photography. She and her husband and two daughters live in the beautiful Shenandoah Valley of Virginia, where they own a toy store, Timeless Toys, and several other businesses. Connect with her at www.hopeful-things.com or on Instagram or Facebook.